D0064020

By the Editors of *WORKBENCH* Magazine

Attention Schools and Business Firms:
KC PUBLISHING books are available at quantity discounts for bulk purchases for education, business or sales promotion use. For more information call our Book Department at (816) 531-5730.

Printed in the United States of America

Library of Congress Cataloguing-in-Publication Data

TOYS TO BUILD

By the Editors of *WORKBENCH* Magazine

ISBN: 0-86675-017-7

Anyone who played with homemade toys as a child understands their sentimental value. Years after the Play-Doh has dried up, the Power Rangers have been entombed in the attic and Barney has been buried at the bottom of the closet, your kids will remember the wooden toys that were made just for them.

Toys to Build has something for everyone — toys that children of all ages will enjoy and projects that woodworkers of all skill levels will have fun making. Some of the projects, such as the periscope, the tic-tac-toe game and the puzzles, are simple enough for beginners and require only a few tools; others, such as the Lotus racer, the steamroller and the steam shovel, are more challenging.

The editors would like to thank the following people for their contributions to *Toys to Build*: David Ashe, F.J. Badeaux, John Decker, R.J. DeCristoforo, Richard Graybill, Jeff Greef, Dave Kraatz and Susan Tower for the design and construction of many of the projects; Clarke Barre, Dyck Fledderus and James P. Sexton for their technical drawings and Scott Cook and Al Surratt for their photos.

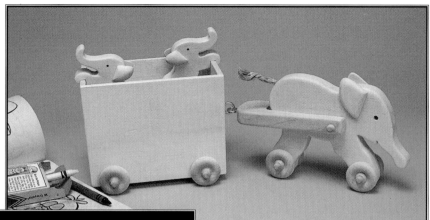

Elephant Cart Page 20

Three Dinosaurs Page 12

**Roll
Rover**
Page 24

Gumball Dispenser
Page 28

Rugged Rig
Page 38

Durable Dollhouse
Page 32

Building Blocks
Page 48

Stack-and-Roll Pull Toy
Page 44

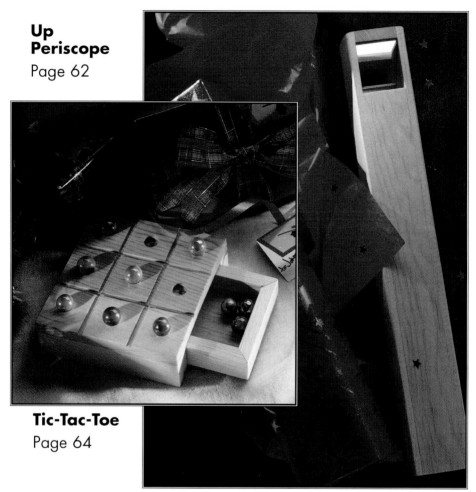

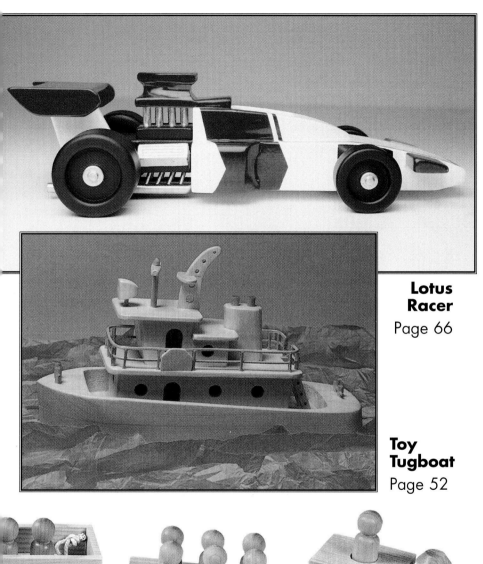

**Lotus
Racer**
Page 66

**Toy
Tugboat**
Page 52

Toy Train
Page 56

Wagon With Blocks
Page 74

Little House on the Prairie
Page 78

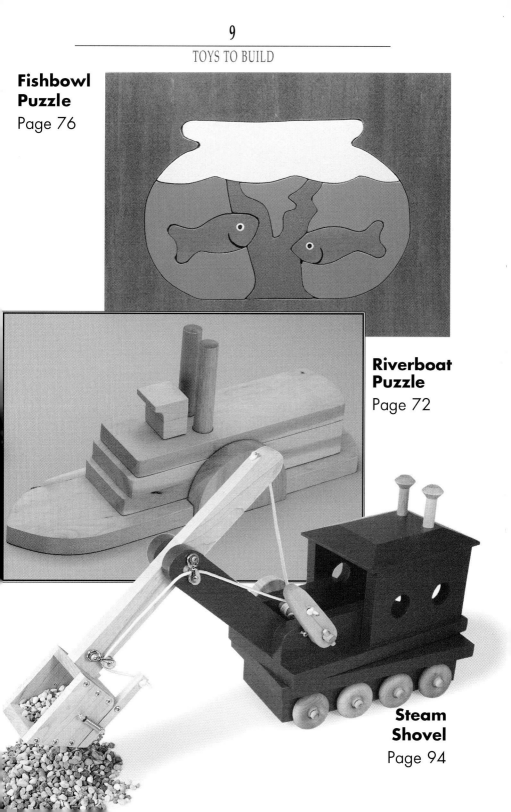

Fishbowl Puzzle
Page 76

Riverboat Puzzle
Page 72

Steam Shovel
Page 94

Little Haulers   Page 80

Steamroller
Page 86

11
TOYS TO BUILD

THREE DINOSAURS

Using the patterns on the following pages, create your own Jurassic pack: a 7-in.-tall x 19-1/2-in.-long triceratops, a 16-in.-long x 19-in.-tall tyrannosaurus and a 9-in.-tall x 16-1/2-in.-long sailback.

ho says dinosaurs are extinct? You can create your own triceratops, Tyrannosaurus rex and sailback dinosaurs using a band saw or scroll saw, glue and sandpaper. Power sanding equipment (a belt/disc sander, drill press, sanding drums, etc.) and a router are optional, but they'll eliminate a lot of hand sanding.

Pine is a good choice for this project because it's inexpensive and easy to work. Consider poplar if you'd like a painted finish, or use mahogany for a more upscale dinosaur. If you can't

THREE DINOSAURS

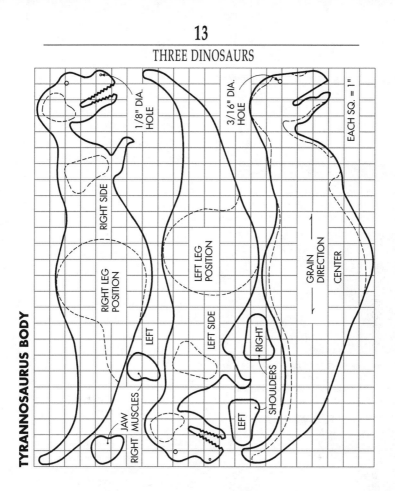

TYRANNOSAURUS BODY

RIGHT SIDE

1/8" DIA. HOLE

3/16" DIA. HOLE

EACH SQ. = 1"

RIGHT LEG POSITION

LEFT LEG POSITION

GRAIN DIRECTION

CENTER

LEFT SIDE

LEFT

RIGHT

SHOULDERS

LEFT

JAW

RIGHT MUSCLES

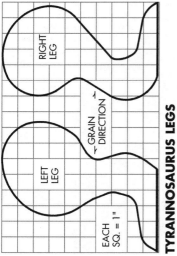

TYRANNOSAURUS LEGS

RIGHT LEG

LEFT LEG

GRAIN DIRECTION

EACH SQ. = 1"

purchase 1/2-in. stock, use 3/4-in. stock and mill it on a thickness planer. No planer? Use the 3/4-in. stock straight off the shelf. Your dinosaurs will simply have more girth.

INSTRUCTIONS FOR ALL

The following instructions apply to all three dinosaurs. Where necessary, some instructions refer to one specific dinosaur.

Enlarge the patterns to full size and use them to trace the shapes onto the stock. Because it's hard to find clear pine these days, you'll probably have to use boards with knots. Arrange the patterns to avoid the worst defects; then trace around the edges of the patterns (photo 1, p. 14). Take special care to lay out parts so the grain runs

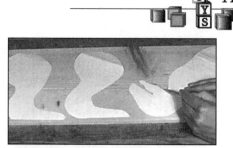

1 Cut out the patterns, then arrange them on the stock to avoid knots on the pattern edges.

2 Some curved parts, such as the dinosaur's neck, are difficult to cut. Relief cuts allow the blade to cut curves without binding.

3 When cutting the teeth, first make a narrow cut across the top of the teeth to the back of the mouth; then cut the saw-tooth pattern.

4 Smooth the edges of the parts with a 1-in. belt sander. Sand hard-to-reach areas by hand.

as indicated on the patterns. The correct grain orientation is also shown in the photos.

Whether you use a band saw or a scroll saw, the time it takes to cut the parts is about the same. A band saw cuts very quickly but leaves a relatively rough edge. That means you'll spend time sanding. A scroll saw doesn't cut as fast, but it cuts smoothly and eliminates the need for all but finish sanding. Also, because of its small blade, a scroll saw can cut tight curves without first making relief cuts. If you have both tools, pick the one you prefer. If not, use what you have — either tool will do a good job.

If you use a band saw, use a narrow blade (1/4 in. is a good size) to cut curves and get into tight corners easier. Blades narrower than

The 1/12-scale pine tyrannosaurus stands about 19 in. high. The original Rex, which lived in the western part of North America during the Cretaceous period, survived by preying on other dinosaurs.

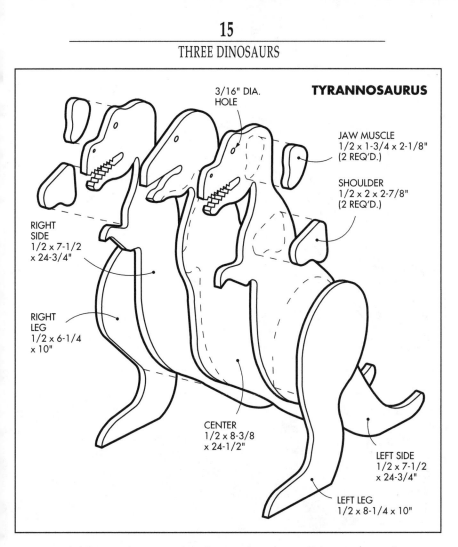

3/16" DIA. HOLE

TYRANNOSAURUS

JAW MUSCLE
1/2 x 1-3/4 x 2-1/8"
(2 REQ'D.)

SHOULDER
1/2 x 2 x 2-7/8"
(2 REQ'D.)

RIGHT SIDE
1/2 x 7-1/2 x 24-3/4"

RIGHT LEG
1/2 x 6-1/4 x 10"

CENTER
1/2 x 8-3/8 x 24-1/2"

LEFT SIDE
1/2 x 7-1/2 x 24-3/4"

LEFT LEG
1/2 x 8-1/4 x 10"

1/4 in. are delicate and prone to breaking. You can spend a lot of time and money changing blades that break because they're too thin. Choose a fine-tooth blade — it will make a smoother cut and save time sanding.

There are some particularly tight cuts below the chin on the tyrannosaurus and between the triceratops' horns. Don't try to cut tight curves and corners in one pass on a band saw. You can break the blade or even pull it off the band saw wheels. Instead, make several parallel cuts into the corner and up to the pattern line (photo 2). Be careful not to pull the blade as you retract the work. Next, follow the pattern line and slowly cut away the waste pieces. When you're finished cutting, sand away any waste that's left along the traced line.

The mouth on the tyrannosaurus is tricky to cut (photo 3). First make a cut to the back, turn off the saw and remove the work. Then begin again, cutting just over the tops of the teeth.

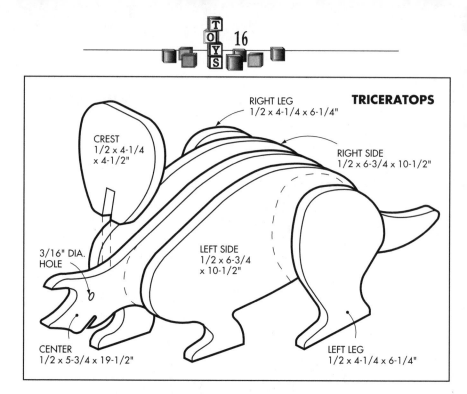

TRICERATOPS

RIGHT LEG
1/2 x 4-1/4 x 6-1/4"

CREST
1/2 x 4-1/4
x 4-1/2"

RIGHT SIDE
1/2 x 6-3/4 x 10-1/2"

3/16" DIA.
HOLE

LEFT SIDE
1/2 x 6-3/4
x 10-1/2"

CENTER
1/2 x 5-3/4 x 19-1/2"

LEFT LEG
1/2 x 4-1/4 x 6-1/4"

You'll need to move the piece back and forth to cut all of the teeth angles.

The 19-1/2-in.-long triceratops is modeled after the original 30-ft. behemoths.

SANDING AND FINISHING

After you have cut out the parts, sand all the edges with 120-grit sandpaper. You can use a 1-in. bench-top belt sander (photo 4) for the outside and large-diameter inside curves. To sand tight corners and curves, use a drill press with sanding drums sized to fit the curves (photo 5, p. 18). You can buy sanding drums at most hardware stores and home centers. Small rasps and files would also do a good job.

For appearance and safety, it's important to smooth all the outside edges. Use a router table and rounding over bit for the larger pieces (photo 6). If you're working with 1/2-in. stock, use a 3/16-in.-radius bit. A 1/4-in.-radius bit is best with 3/4-in. stock. If you don't have a router, round the edges with rasps, files or sandpaper.

Round both sides of the center pieces except where they meet or are overlapped by the edges of the sides. Avoid rounding in these areas by marking them with the pattern. Don't round too much on the first edge or the router bit's pilot bearing won't have a face to ride on when you rout the second edge.

The shoulders and jaw muscles on the tyrannosaurus are too small to rout safely. Instead, round the edges of these pieces with a sander or a rasp; then sand the edges.

Before assembly, mark the location of each part on the underlying layer. To keep the parts from sliding around during assembly, apply glue and let them stand for a few minutes to allow the glue to become tacky before joining them.

Use small wood blocks to keep the clamp jaws from denting the wood (photo 7). Align the feet on

TRICERATOPS

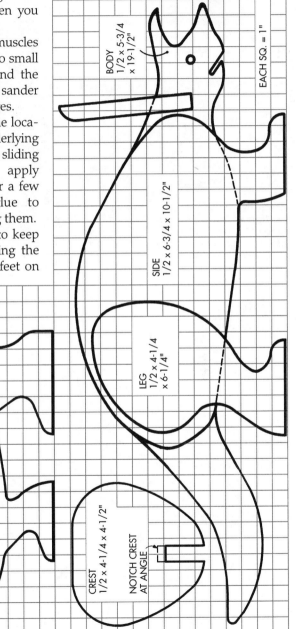

BODY 1/2 x 5-3/4 x 19-1/2"

EACH SQ. = 1"

SIDE 1/2 x 6-3/4 x 10-1/2"

LEG 1/2 x 4-1/2 x 6-1/4"

LEG 1/2 x 4-1/4 x 6-1/4"

SIDE 1/2 x 6-3/4 x 10-1/2"

CREST 1/2 x 4-1/4 x 4-1/2"

NOTCH CREST AT ANGLE

5 Use a small drum sander to remove saw blade marks from tight corners.

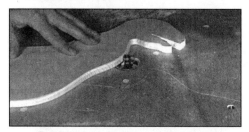

6 Round both edges of the center section — except where the sides meet the center — and the outside edge of the legs and sides with a 3/16-in. rounding over bit in a router table.

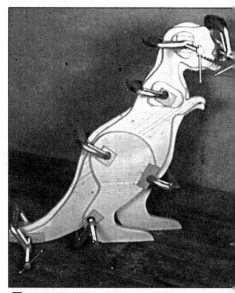

7 Spread glue evenly with a brush, then clamp for at least an hour.

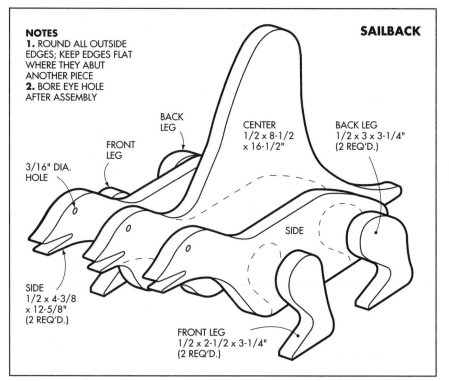

SAILBACK

NOTES
1. ROUND ALL OUTSIDE EDGES; KEEP EDGES FLAT WHERE THEY ABUT ANOTHER PIECE
2. BORE EYE HOLE AFTER ASSEMBLY

BACK LEG

FRONT LEG

CENTER
1/2 x 8-1/2 x 16-1/2"

BACK LEG
1/2 x 3 x 3-1/4"
(2 REQ'D.)

3/16" DIA. HOLE

SIDE

SIDE
1/2 x 4-3/8 x 12-5/8"
(2 REQ'D.)

FRONT LEG
1/2 x 2-1/2 x 3-1/4"
(2 REQ'D.)

Sailback dinosaurs — both herbivorous and carnivorous — roamed prehistoric earth. We'd like to think that this docile-looking creature was a herbivore.

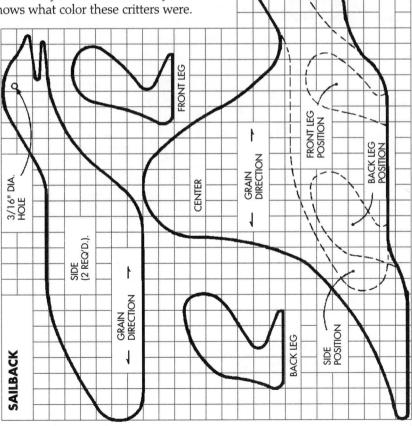

the triceratops and the feet and tail on the tyrannosaurus and sailback so they can stand up.

Now drill holes for the eyes and nostrils and finish with a few coats of varnish or enamel. Any color would be okay — no one knows what color these critters were.

EACH SQ. = 1"

FRONT LEG

3/16" DIA. HOLE

SIDE (2 REQ'D.).

CENTER

GRAIN DIRECTION

GRAIN DIRECTION

FRONT LEG POSITION

BACK LEG POSITION

BACK LEG

SIDE POSITION

SAILBACK

ELEPHANT CART

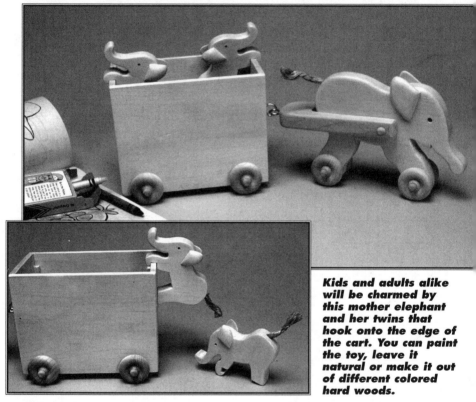

Kids and adults alike will be charmed by this mother elephant and her twins that hook onto the edge of the cart. You can paint the toy, leave it natural or make it out of different colored hard woods.

t's said that an elephant never forgets — at least to take the kids when she goes to the grocery store. With this elephant and cart design, the mother elephant (or an imaginative child) can do just that. You can make it possible using just a table saw and a scroll saw or band saw. A router and drill press are also helpful.

There is quite a bit of sanding to do on this project, so pine is a good choice because it sands easily. However, you might prefer to use a hard wood such as walnut for its color. Building this project is a good way to use up any scraps you have left over from past projects.

MAKING ELEPHANTS

Enlarge the elephant patterns to full size (a photocopier works best) and trace them onto 3/4-in.-thick stock. Cut out the elephants with a

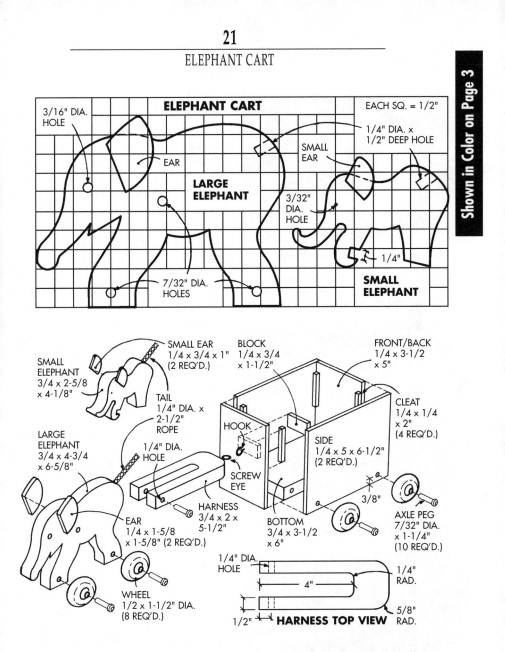

ELEPHANT CART

EACH SQ. = 1/2"

3/16" DIA. HOLE

1/4" DIA. x 1/2" DEEP HOLE

EAR

SMALL EAR

LARGE ELEPHANT

3/32" DIA. HOLE

1/4"

7/32" DIA. HOLES

SMALL ELEPHANT

SMALL EAR 1/4 x 3/4 x 1" (2 REQ'D.)

BLOCK 1/4 x 3/4 x 1-1/2"

FRONT/BACK 1/4 x 3-1/2 x 5"

SMALL ELEPHANT 3/4 x 2-5/8 x 4-1/8"

TAIL 1/4" DIA. x 2-1/2" ROPE

HOOK

CLEAT 1/4 x 1/4 x 2" (4 REQ'D.)

LARGE ELEPHANT 3/4 x 4-3/4 x 6-5/8"

1/4" DIA. HOLE

SIDE 1/4 x 5 x 6-1/2" (2 REQ'D.)

SCREW EYE

3/8"

AXLE PEG 7/32" DIA. x 1-1/4" (10 REQ'D.)

EAR 1/4 x 1-5/8 x 1-5/8" (2 REQ'D.)

HARNESS 3/4 x 2 x 5-1/2"

BOTTOM 3/4 x 3-1/2 x 6"

WHEEL 1/2 x 1-1/2" DIA. (8 REQ'D.)

1/4" DIA. HOLE

1/4" RAD.

4"

5/8" RAD.

1/2" **HARNESS TOP VIEW**

band saw or a scroll saw (photo 1, p. 22). A scroll saw works best for small parts with tight curves like these. Use a 1/4- or 1/8-in.-wide blade with a band saw. Be careful not to pull the blade off the band saw wheels when you are backing out of a cut. Turn off the saw if the blade binds.

Sand the edges smooth by hand with 150-grit sandpaper or with a small drum sander mounted in the drill press. These drum sanders are available at most hardware stores and home centers.

1 *Use a fine-tooth scroll saw blade to cut out the elephant. It will help reduce sanding and make it easier to negotiate tight curves while cutting.*

2 *Round over the edge of the large (mother) elephant on the router table with a bearing-guided bit. Keep your fingers as far from the bit as possible.*

3 *Sand or plane the cart sides smooth. Use a bench dog or a stop on the end of the bench to prevent the work from being thrown by the belt sander.*

Round over the edges of the mother elephant with sandpaper, or use a router table and a 1/8-in. rounding over bit (photo 2). The baby elephants, however, are too small for you to safely make using the router table, so sand the edges by hand. Wait to drill the holes for the tails, eyes and wheel axles until you drill the axle holes in the cart.

MAKING THIN STOCK

Make 1/4-in.-thick stock for the cart sides and elephant ears by resawing 3/4-in.-thick x 5-in.-wide stock on the table saw or band saw. (Of course, you can redesign the project to use off-the-shelf stock and eliminate resawing.) For safety's sake, the stock should be at least 18 in. long and straight so that it won't bind in the saw blade. Be sure to use a pushstick.

If you use a table saw, make resaw cuts in successive passes. First, raise the blade to 1-1/4 in. and set the rip fence 1/4 in. from the blade. Make four cuts: two on each edge and one on each face. Raise the blade to 2-5/8 in.; then duplicate the cuts to separate both pieces and bring them to thickness. Always keep your fingers above the blade for safety.

Remove the saw marks from the inside faces of the boards with a hand plane or a belt sander (photo 3). It's not as important for the boards to be exactly 1/4 in. thick as it is for them to be smooth and consistent in thickness. Cut the cart sides to length using the miter gauge on the table saw (photo 4).

ASSEMBLING THE CART

Glue together the cart sides and bottom. Let glue soak into the end

ELEPHANT CART

grain for a minute or two before you assemble the parts; then clamp. Glued end grain is weak, so for additional strength, glue and clamp 1/4- x 1/4- x 2-in. cleats into the cart corners. Use C-clamps and minimal clamping pressure to prevent denting the corners.

Before boring the axle holes, be sure you have a drill bit that matches the diameter of the axle pegs. Drill test holes to confirm this.

Use the drill press to bore axle holes in the cart sides (photo 5). If you don't have a drill press, first mark and punch the holes; then put the cart in a vise and bore the holes with a hand drill. Bore holes for the wheels, tail and eyes.

Glue the axle pegs in place with the wheels (photo 6). Put glue in the hole and wipe a little on the peg as well.

Shorten the mother elephant's wheel and yoke axles to prevent them from hitting inside the axle holes. Use glue sparingly on these pegs and holes as well. Apply glue to the hole; then wipe out as much as you can with a sliver, toothpick or nail. Wipe excess glue off the axle pegs.

Cut out the ears from 1/4-in. stock using a scroll saw. Roughly round over the edges and glue them in place; then sand them smooth. For the tails, unravel a strand of 1/4-in.-dia. rope.

Glue a 1/4-in.-thick x 1-in.-sq. piece of stock onto the inside of the cart behind the screw eye to give the threads more bite. Widen the eye on the cart so that the yoke and cart can be unhitched. Mother elephant likes toting the kids around, but there are times when she needs to get away.

4 Screw an auxiliary wood fence to your table saw's miter gauge to add support when crosscutting the cart sides and other short pieces.

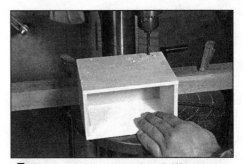

5 Clamp a fence to the drill press table to ensure uniform spacing of the axle holes from the bottom of the cart.

6 Glue the axles to the cart with the wheels mounted. Don't use too much glue or the squeeze-out will bond the wheels to the axles and prevent them from turning.

ROLL ROVER

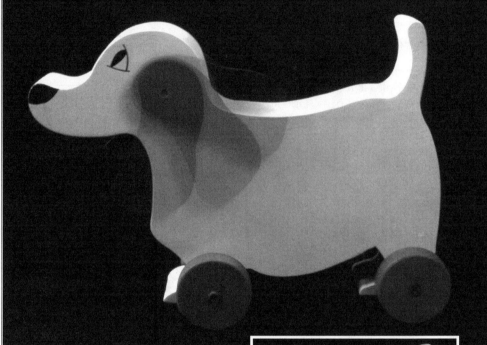

ABOVE: Young children will enjoy walking this dog, whose bright-colored ears swing as he rolls obediently behind.
RIGHT: The rear axle, which activates the ear cam, is bent into a U shape where the connecting rod is attached.

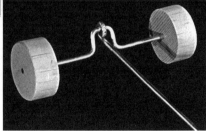

Give this pooch a push and watch his ears rock as he rolls. You don't have to be an engineer to build this animated animal, but it helps if you're not too old to learn a few new tricks.

The dog's ears, which swing back and forth as he glides across the floor, are moved by a simple cam mechanism (see drawings) that operates in a cavity in the body. The body is made of three layers of 3/4-in. stock, which are glued together after the cam

ROLL ROVER

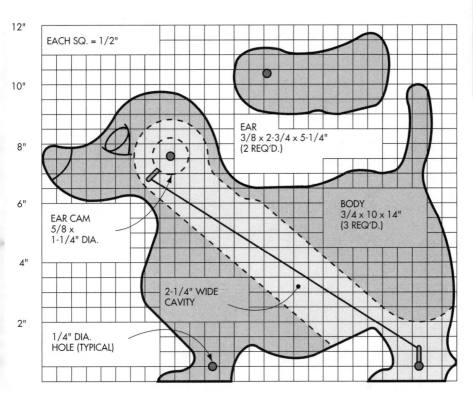

EACH SQ. = 1/2"

EAR
3/8 x 2-3/4 x 5-1/4"
(2 REQ'D.)

BODY
3/4 x 10 x 14"
(3 REQ'D.)

EAR CAM
5/8 x
1-1/4" DIA.

2-1/4" WIDE
CAVITY

1/4" DIA.
HOLE (TYPICAL)

mechanism has been assembled.

Begin by enlarging the grid pattern to full size using a photocopier or drawing the pattern on graph paper with 1/2-in. squares. Trace the full-size pattern onto one of the pieces; then clamp all three pieces together and cut the shape with a band saw. (You could also use a scroll saw or sabre saw, but you probably won't be able to cut all three layers at once.)

Next, lay out the cavity for the ear cam mechanism on the middle layer and cut it out. Clamp the two outside layers together and bore the through-

holes for the ear and wheel axles. Sand all edges smooth.

INTERNAL ORGANS

Cut the 1-1/4-in.-dia. ear cam from 5/8-in.-thick stock using a hole saw. The hole saw will bore a 1/4-in.-dia. hole through the center for the dowel that acts as the ear axle. Insert the 1/4-in.-dia. dowel through the cam and glue it in place; then attach the 3/8-in. screw eye to the cam.

Clamp the middle layer to one of the outside layers so you can mount the cam and the rear axle. This will allow you to determine the exact

length of the connecting rod. Fasten the wire connecting rod to the screw eye and the rear axle by bending loops on both ends of the rod. Check that there is sufficient clearance for the parts to function correctly. When you are satisfied that the action is smooth, glue and clamp the three layers together. When the glue is dry, sand the entire body smooth.

ADDING EARS AND WHEELS

To make two identical ears, resaw a 3/4-in.-thick piece into two 3/8-in.-thick pieces using a band saw. Then trace the ear pattern onto one of the pieces, clamp both pieces together and cut them to shape. While the pieces are still clamped together, bore a through-hole for the ear axle.

Cut the wheels with a hole saw. The holes made by the hole saw in the front wheels will be the right size for the dowel axle, but you'll need to plug the holes in the rear wheels and then bore smaller ones for the axle rod. It's essential that the rear wheels fit tightly on the axle, so bore test holes in a scrap piece to determine the correct hole diameter for the rod you're using.

Paint the body, ears and wheels before you assemble them. When the paint is dry, glue the ears and the wheels onto the axles. You should use

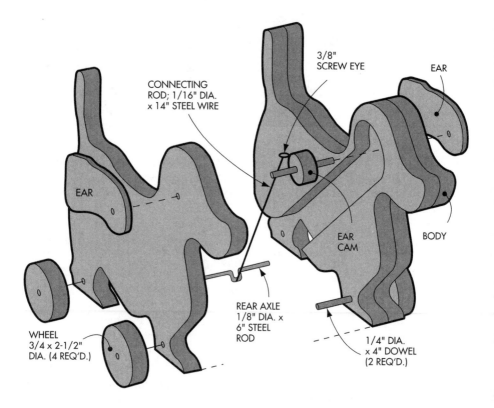

ROLL ROVER

yellow glue for the ears and front wheels and epoxy glue for the rear wheels. Put washers on the axles to keep the moving parts from rubbing on the body. Finally, drive a screw eye in the center front of the dog's neck and attach a piece of string for a leash. Your dog is ready to roll.

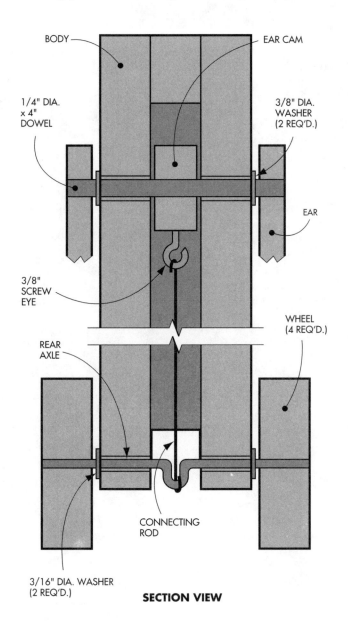

BODY

EAR CAM

1/4" DIA.
x 4"
DOWEL

3/8" DIA.
WASHER
(2 REQ'D.)

EAR

3/8"
SCREW
EYE

WHEEL
(4 REQ'D.)

REAR
AXLE

CONNECTING
ROD

3/16" DIA. WASHER
(2 REQ'D.)

SECTION VIEW

GUMBALL DISPENSER

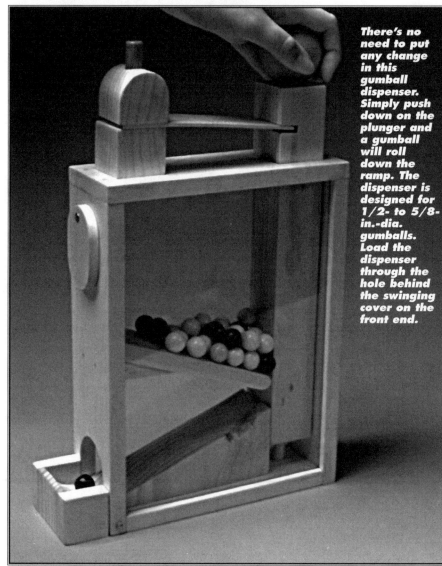

There's no need to put any change in this gumball dispenser. Simply push down on the plunger and a gumball will roll down the ramp. The dispenser is designed for 1/2- to 5/8-in.-dia. gumballs. Load the dispenser through the hole behind the swinging cover on the front end.

GUMBALL DISPENSER

f you've ever watched helplessly as a vending machine took your money and left your nacho-cheese-flavored pork rinds hanging from the mechanism that's supposed to dispense the goods, this gumball dispenser may be just what you need. Its mechanism is simple to build and reliable. And if it should fail to work, you can shake the dickens out of the dispenser without worrying about a twitchy security guard investigating. Of course, it is a great gift for youngsters (although dentists might beg to differ).

TOOLS AND MATERIALS

To build the dispenser you'll need a table saw or radial arm saw, a drill, a scroll saw or sabre saw and a few hand tools. Optional tools include a belt sander, router, planer, hole saw and band saw. Don't hesitate to substitute any other tools that you feel more comfortable using.

Most of the wood parts are pine except for the spring, handle and dowels. However, you can make the project with almost any wood you like. The sides are 3/32-in. clear acrylic, but you can substitute 1/8-in.-thick material. Just be sure that you can fit the plastic into the grooves in the top, ends and bottom.

Because the parts are various thicknesses, you'll need to saw or plane them from thicker stock unless you can find the right sizes at your lumber supplier. Remember that for the dis-penser to fit together and work, the parts must be made accurately.

MAKING PARTS

The easiest way to make the bottom **A**, top **B** and ends **C** is to start with one 1/2- x 3- x 36-in. board. First, cut the two grooves for the sides **D** using a table saw with a 1/8-in.-kerf blade; then cut the parts out.

Lay out the openings in the top and front end; then use a scroll saw or sabre saw to cut them out. Bore the pilot holes in both ends **C** for no. 6 x 1-1/4-in. flathead wood screws to attach the bottom during assembly (see drawing, pp. 30-31).

Cut the cover **E** with a scroll saw or use a belt sander to round the corners on square stock. Bore an oversize pilot hole in the cover so it can swing back and forth when it's screwed in place.

Next, transfer the pattern for the ramp **F** to the stock and cut it out with a scroll saw or sabre saw. Be sure to sand the top of the ramp smooth and flat. Notch the top edge of the ramp as shown in the drawing with a pocketknife or chisel. This makes a flat spot for gumballs to hit when they drop from the plunger. You may need to adjust the size and shape of the notch when you assemble the parts.

Glue the chute brace **H** and chute **I** together; then glue and nail the assembly to the front end.

The spring **L** may need to be a little thicker or thinner than what's

CUTTING LIST:
GUMBALL DISPENSER
(all parts pine except as noted)

Key	No.	Part, Mat'l.	Size
A	1	Bottom	1/2 x 3 x 7"
B	1	Top	1/2 x 3 x 8"
C	2	Ends	1/2 x 3 x 10"
D	2	Sides, Clear acrylic	3/32 x 7-1/4 x 9-3/4"
E	1	Cover	3/8 x 1-3/4 x 2-1/2"
F	1	Ramp	1-3/4 x 2-3/4 x 7-1/4"
G	2	Ramp sides	1/2 x 1-1/2 x 1-1/2"
H	1	Chute brace	5/8 x 2 x 1-7/8"
I	1	Chute	1/2 x 2-1/8 x 5-1/2"
J	1	Spring block	1-3/8 x 1-1/2 x 1-5/8"
K	1	Spring block cap	1-1/2 x 1-1/2 x 1-5/8"
L	1	Spring, Maple or birch	1/8 x 1-1/2 x 5-3/4"
M	1	Plunger	1-5/8 x 1-3/4 x 11-3/8"
N	1	Handle, Birch ball	2" dia.

Misc.: No. 6 x 3/4" FHWS (1); no. 6 x 1-1/4" FHWS (4); no. 8 x 1-1/2" FHWS (4); no. 8 x 2" FHWS (1); 1-1/4" finishing nails (6); 1/8" dia. x 1/2" dowel; 3/8" dia. x 1-1/2" dowel; 3/8" dia. x 2" dowel; 1/2" dia. x 1-3/4" dowel; yellow glue; wood putty; 5/8" dia. gumballs.

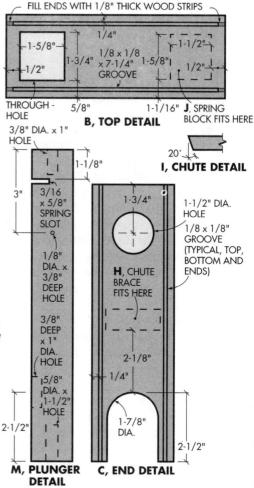

called for in the cutting list, and because it can weaken and bend, you may want to make some extras. Bore the pilot hole and counterbore in the spring block cap **K**. Put the spring block **J**, the spring and the spring block cap together and bore the pilot hole for the no. 8 x 2-in. flathead wood screw through the spring and spring block. Then screw all three together.

Bore the holes in the top and bottom of the plunger **M** and the bottom of the handle **N**. The bottom hole in the plunger fits loosely over the dowel in the bottom **A** because it guides the plunger's vertical movement. Next, cut the 3/16- x 5/8-in. slot in the side of the plunger where the spring is retained and bore the gumball-pickup hole in the side of the plunger. Round over the edges of the hole so the gumballs will roll out easily.

ASSEMBLY

It's important to note that although most of the parts are glued and nailed together, the bottom is screwed on. This allows you to occasionally clean or repair the dispenser if necessary.

First, glue the 3/8-in. dowels to the

GUMBALL DISPENSER

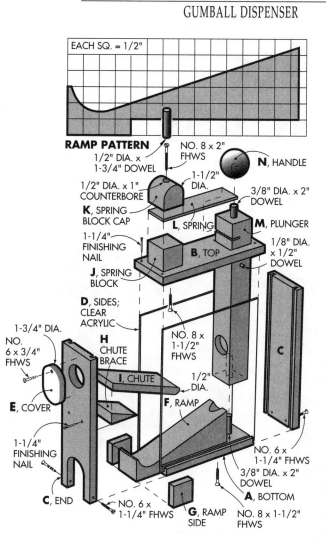

EACH SQ. = 1/2"

RAMP PATTERN

NO. 8 x 2" FHWS

1/2" DIA. x 1-3/4" DOWEL

N, HANDLE

1/2" DIA. x 1" COUNTERBORE

1-1/2" DIA.

3/8" DIA. x 2" DOWEL

K, SPRING BLOCK CAP

L, SPRING

M, PLUNGER

1-1/4" FINISHING NAIL

B, TOP

1/8" DIA. x 1/2" DOWEL

J, SPRING BLOCK

D, SIDES; CLEAR ACRYLIC

1-3/4" DIA. NO. 6 x 3/4" FHWS

H CHUTE BRACE

NO. 8 x 1-1/2" FHWS

C

I, CHUTE

1/2" DIA.

E, COVER

F, RAMP

1-1/4" FINISHING NAIL

NO. 6 x 1-1/4" FHWS

3/8" DIA. x 2" DOWEL

A, BOTTOM

C, END

NO. 6 x 1-1/4" FHWS

G, RAMP SIDE

NO. 8 x 1-1/2" FHWS

glue and 1-1/4-in. finishing nails. (The chute and chute brace should already be glued and nailed to the front end.) Put the acrylic sides in the grooves to help align the parts while assembling. Now screw on the bottom and you're ready to check the mechanism.

Turn the spring out of the way so you can insert the plunger; then capture the spring in the plunger's slot. Put a few gumballs in the machine and press down on the plunger to check that only one gumball at a time is dispensed. When you're satisfied with the operation, complete the assembly.

Disassemble the dispenser and glue the 1/8-in. stop dowel in the plunger; then push the plunger up through the top and recapture the spring. Assemble the remainder of the parts as you did before; then glue on the handle **N**. Now you can glue on the ramp sides **G** and screw on the cover **E**. Finally, fill all the nail holes with wood putty and sand the putty flush when it's dry.

The dispenser shown in the photo was left unfinished, but it would look great with a colorful enamel paint job.

top of the plunger and the bottom **A**. Next, screw the ramp **F** to the bottom so the notch on the underside of the ramp fits snugly against the front of the bottom. Glue and screw the spring block assembly to the top **B**. (Don't glue the dowel in the top of the spring block cap; leave it loose so you can unscrew the block to adjust or replace the spring.)

Assemble the top and ends with

DURABLE DOLLHOUSE

Good-quality 3/8-in. plywood and neat assembly make this no-frills dollhouse durable, attractive and free of splinters. It measures about 15 in. deep x 23 in. high x 33 in. long.

ven if you had time to build a fancy dollhouse for your toddlers, there isn't enough hot glue in the world to keep it together. The dollhouse you see here, however, is likely to hold up through several generations.

This dollhouse is designed to be played with, not set out for display. What it lacks in detail, it makes up for in durability. Its large, simple rooms

DURABLE DOLLHOUSE

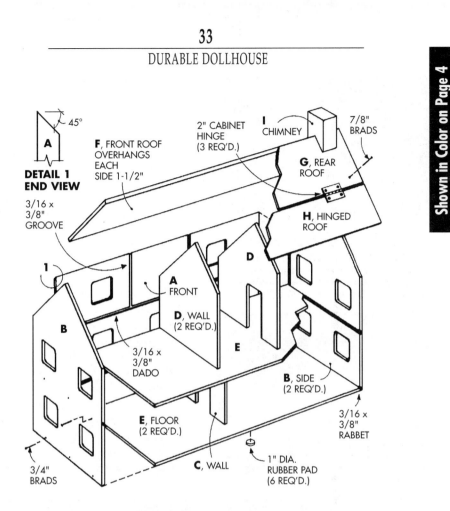

DETAIL 1
END VIEW

45°

A

3/16 x 3/8" GROOVE

F, FRONT ROOF OVERHANGS EACH SIDE 1-1/2"

2" CABINET HINGE (3 REQ'D.)

I CHIMNEY

7/8" BRADS

G, REAR ROOF

H, HINGED ROOF

D

A FRONT

D, WALL (2 REQ'D.)

3/16 x 3/8" DADO

E

B, SIDE (2 REQ'D.)

B

3/16 x 3/8" RABBET

E, FLOOR (2 REQ'D.)

C, WALL

1" DIA. RUBBER PAD (6 REQ'D.)

3/4" BRADS

and smoothly finished corners make it perfect for young children, and spacious window and door openings are just the right size for small hands to reach through comfortably.

A PLYWOOD FORTRESS

Canadian birch plywood gives this durable dollhouse its strength. With seven void-free layers, the plywood is strong and warp resistant. It also has two smooth sides, so you can paint it if you want to. Similar plywoods such as ApplePly or any high-quality European plywood would also work.

Begin your dollhouse by using the patterns on p. 35 to lay out and cut all of the plywood pieces to size. Cut the floors and roof pieces as well. If you're using a table saw, use a plywood blade with at least 60 teeth to avoid chipping. You can also cut the pieces using a sabre saw with a fine-tooth plywood-cutting blade. In either instance, you should score the layout lines with a utility knife or hobby knife to minimize chipping.

WINDOW/DOOR JIG

To cut smooth, uniform window and door openings, use a homemade router jig (see photo 1 and accompa-

1 Align the jig with the layout lines for the cutouts and clamp the jig down. Move the pattern bit clockwise around the jig.

2 After cutting all of the openings and joints, sand the parts on both faces to remove splinters and to smooth the surfaces.

WINDOW/DOOR JIG

CLAMPING TAB
1 x 1-3/4 x 2"
(2 REQ'D.)

1-1/2"

SIDE 1 x 2 x 22"
(2 REQ'D.)

2"

7"

2"

SPACER
1 x 3 x 4"

3"

4"

3"

2"

NO. 8 x
2-1/2" FHWS

1"

SPACER
1 x 2 x 3"
(2 REQ'D.)

3"

nying drawing) and a 1/2-in.-dia. pattern-cutting bit in a router. The maple jig has a 3-in.-wide opening for the doors and windows. The jig provides an edge for the bit's bearing to ride on as it cuts the openings. You can't plunge a pattern-cutting bit into the stock, so cut 1-in.-dia. entry holes for the bit in all of the window areas. The door opening of the jig is 1 in. longer than the actual 6-in.-long door openings. This allows the router

3 Draw layout lines on the outside faces of the sides and front to indicate the centerline of the grooves and dadoes; then glue and nail the sides to the floors. Next, attach the front with glue and nails.

All of the joints and openings have been cut and the parts are ready for assembly. The router jig at the bottom right lets you cut openings with smooth edges.

DURABLE DOLLHOUSE

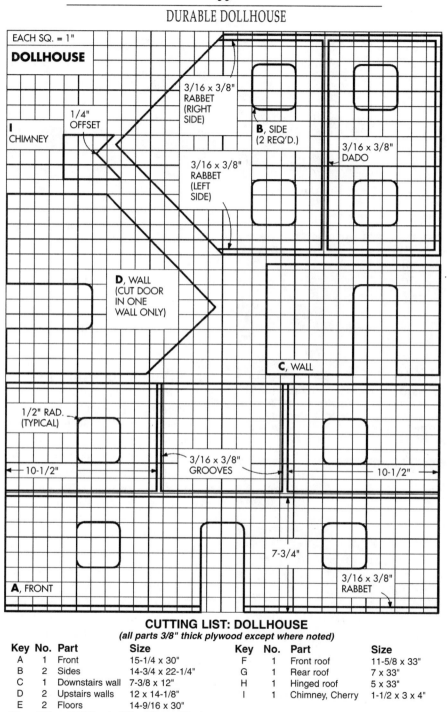

EACH SQ. = 1"

DOLLHOUSE

3/16 x 3/8"
RABBET
(RIGHT
SIDE)

1/4"
OFFSET

I
CHIMNEY

B, SIDE
(2 REQ'D.)

3/16 x 3/8"
DADO

3/16 x 3/8"
RABBET
(LEFT
SIDE)

D, WALL
(CUT DOOR
IN ONE
WALL ONLY)

C, WALL

1/2" RAD.
(TYPICAL)

3/16 x 3/8"
GROOVES

10-1/2"

10-1/2"

7-3/4"

3/16 x 3/8"
RABBET

A, FRONT

CUTTING LIST: DOLLHOUSE
(all parts 3/8" thick plywood except where noted)

Key	No.	Part	Size	Key	No.	Part	Size
A	1	Front	15-1/4 x 30"	F	1	Front roof	11-5/8 x 33"
B	2	Sides	14-3/4 x 22-1/4"	G	1	Rear roof	7 x 33"
C	1	Downstairs wall	7-3/8 x 12"	H	1	Hinged roof	5 x 33"
D	2	Upstairs walls	12 x 14-1/8"	I	1	Chimney, Cherry	1-1/2 x 3 x 4"
E	2	Floors	14-9/16 x 30"				

Misc.: 3/4" and 7/8" brads; 2" butt hinges (3); glue.

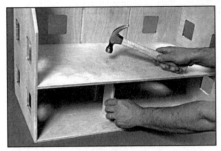

4 Glue and nail the downstairs wall C to the floors. Use a layout line if you need to.

5 Next, install the upstairs walls in the grooves in the front. A nail through the floor into the bottom edge of each wall holds it in place until you install the roof.

6 Nail the front roof panel to the front — note the layout lines that indicate the center edge of the front and the side. Use a nail set to avoid denting the panel with the hammer.

7 A few dabs of glue should hold the chimney in place.

bit to start at the edge of the plywood, so drilling an entry hole in the doors isn't necessary. Clamping tabs on the jig allow the router to run around the bottom window opening without hitting the clamps.

GROOVES AND RABBETS

Cut the dadoes, the grooves and the rabbets on a router table using a 3/8-in. spiral fluted bit. First, cut all the rabbets in the front **A** and sides **B** — remember that there is a right side and a left side, so the joints should be mirror images of each other — then adjust the router table fence to cut the dadoes for the upstairs floor **E** in the front and sides. Cut the two grooves for the upstairs walls **D** in the front.

Once you've cut all the openings and joints, round the edges by sanding thoroughly (photo 2). If you don't use a vibrating sander before assembly, you'll have to sand by hand after the dollhouse has been glued together.

ASSEMBLY

Begin assembling the dollhouse by gluing and nailing the floors **E** to the sides **B** using 3/4-in. brads (photo 3).

KID-PROOF FURNITURE

A durable dollhouse needs equally durable furniture. Everything shown in the photo is made from scraps. It's hardly exacting work. You can scale the pieces to fit any dolls. The trick is to be creative.

The refrigerator is a scrap piece of 1-1/2- x 2-1/2- x 5-in. maple. The door is made by cutting a kerf all the way around the 1-1/2-in. edge about 1/4 in. from the front with a fine-tooth saw. To turn a 2x2 block of cherry into a kitchen counter, cut kerfs as described above and bore a few holes with a 1/2-in. brad-point drill bit for the stove. A 35mm (1-3/8-in.) x 3/8-in.-deep hole bored with a Forstner bit makes a pretty good sink.

The bed is made from 3/8-in. plywood scraps left over from the dollhouse. The 4-in-wide headboard and footboard are dadoed to accept the rather hard plywood mattress. (The dolls never complain.) The toilet is nothing more than a wooden knob sanded flat on top. The tank is made from a scrap of cherry. It's not American Standard, but it will last just the same.

Glue holds the furniture together.

Attach the front; then glue and nail the downstairs wall C in place (photo 4) before gluing and nailing the upstairs walls D in their grooves (photo 5).

Glue and nail the front roof F in place next. Use 7/8-in. brads to nail the roof to the front, making sure to drive in these brads parallel to the front, not at an angle (photo 6).

After nailing the rear roof G in place, carefully sand all of the outside corners and edges smooth with 120-grit sandpaper. Next, set all the nails and fill the holes with wood putty. Finish-sand all surfaces of the dollhouse with 180-grit sandpaper. Before attaching the hinged roof H, glue the chimney I in place (photo 7). Finish the house with at least three coats of polyurethane. Sand after each coat.

After installing the roof hinges you'll find that the hinge screws protrude slightly through the panels, so be sure to file the tips of the screws flush. All that's left is to nail six rubber pads to the underside of the dollhouse and you're done.

RUGGED RIG

he semi and van shown in the photos below combine to be a formidable transportation fantasy for any youngster. You can build them out of pine or hard wood scraps and make the wheels out of particleboard or buy them ready-made.

CUTTING THE PARTS

Start by ripping a pine 1x8 (3/4 x 7-1/2 in. actual size) to 5-1/2 in. wide for the chassis A, riser B and cab front/back E. Crosscut the chassis to length; then lay out the 3/8-in.-deep x 3/4-in.-wide dadoes that house

The cab has a wide seat and a small wheel on a dowel.

The toy is 3-1/2 ft. long. If you improvise on the basic design for the van's chassis, you can create a flatbed trailer by replacing the van body with railings. Use 1/2-in.-dia. dowels for posts and 1/4- x 3/4-in. lattice for rails. The bumper of the semi is covered with adhesive-backed chrome tape found at an automotive store.

A pattern for the axle blocks is provided in the drawing, p. 40.

the cab. Plow the dadoes with a dado set on your table saw or use a router with a straight mortising bit. If you use a router, clamp a straightedge to guide it.

Round the back corners of the chassis with a sabre saw and file and sand the corners smooth. Cut the riser **B** to length; then use the chassis as a pattern and round all four corners of the riser. Attach the riser to the chassis with glue and 1-1/4-in. finishing nails driven up through the bottom of the chassis.

The axle blocks **C** should be made of maple, which is more durable than pine. Cut the blocks to size; then bore a 3/8-in.-dia. through-hole. If you don't have a drill bit long enough to penetrate the 5-1/2-in.-long block, you'll have to bore at least halfway through from each end. Make sure to accurately mark the drill entry point — dead center — on both ends of the blocks.

Next, use the pattern in the drawing to cut the arcs in the axle blocks. Glue and screw the front axle blocks to the chassis (see drawing, p. 40).

Cut the fender mounts **D** to size and glue and nail them to the chassis. The front ends of the mounts abut the front axle block. Now fasten the remaining axle blocks in place with glue and screws.

BUILDING THE CAB

Cut the cab front/back **E** to length; then cut the front and back windshield openings with a sabre saw. Bore the hole for the steering wheel column in the cab front (see drawing, Steering Wheel Detail); then install the cab parts **E** in the chassis dadoes with glue and nails.

Use the side-view seat pattern to

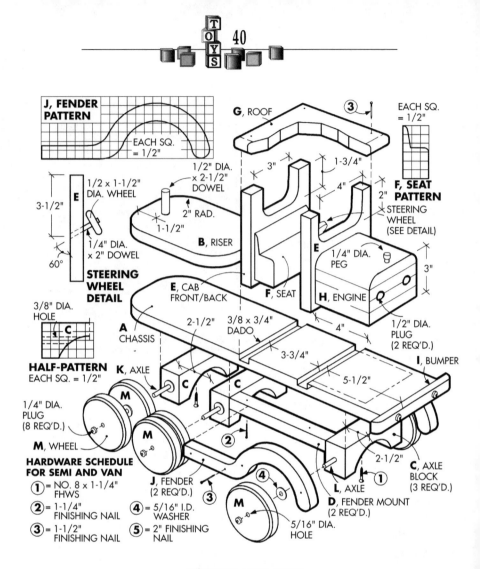

J, FENDER PATTERN — EACH SQ. = 1/2"

G, ROOF — EACH SQ. = 1/2"

F, SEAT PATTERN

1/2 x 1-1/2" DIA. WHEEL — E — 3-1/2"

1/2" DIA. x 2-1/2" DOWEL

2" RAD.

1-1/2"

3" 1-3/4" 4" 2"

STEERING WHEEL (SEE DETAIL)

1/4" DIA. x 2" DOWEL

60°

STEERING WHEEL DETAIL

3/8" DIA. HOLE

HALF-PATTERN EACH SQ. = 1/2"

1/4" DIA. PLUG (8 REQ'D.)

M, WHEEL

HARDWARE SCHEDULE FOR SEMI AND VAN
- ① = NO. 8 x 1-1/4" FHWS
- ② = 1-1/4" FINISHING NAIL
- ③ = 1-1/2" FINISHING NAIL
- ④ = 5/16" I.D. WASHER
- ⑤ = 2" FINISHING NAIL

C

A, CHASSIS

B, RISER

E, CAB FRONT/BACK

F, SEAT

H, ENGINE

2-1/2" 3/8 x 3/4" DADO

3-3/4"

K, AXLE

M

M

1/4" DIA. PEG

1/2" DIA. PLUG (2 REQ'D.)

3"

4"

5-1/2"

I, BUMPER

J, FENDER (2 REQ'D.)

L, AXLE

D, FENDER MOUNT (2 REQ'D.)

5/16" DIA. HOLE

2-1/2"

C, AXLE BLOCK (3 REQ'D.)

CUTTING LIST: SEMI
(all parts pine except where noted)

Key	No.	Part, Mat'l.	Size	Key	No.	Part, Mat'l.	Size
A	1	Chassis	3/4 x 5-1/2 x 20-1/2"	I	1	Bumper	1/2 x 3/4 x 7-1/4"
B	1	Riser	3/4 x 5-1/2 x 8"	J	2	Fenders	3/4 x 3-1/8 x 9-3/4"
C	3	Axle blocks, Maple	1-1/2 x 2 x 5-1/2"	K	2	Axles, Birch dowels	5/16" dia. x 8-5/8"
D	2	Fender mounts	3/4 x 1 x 7-1/2"	L	1	Axle, Birch dowel	5/16" dia. x 7"
E	2	Cab front/back	3/4 x 5-1/2 x 6"	M	10	Wheels, Hard wood or particleboard	3/4" x 3-1/2" dia.
F	1	Seat	1-1/2 x 3 x 4-3/4"				
G	1	Roof	3/4 x 6 x 6-1/2"				
H	1	Engine	3 x 4 x 4-1/2"*				

*Stack and glue four 3/4" thick pine boards together to get the 3" thickness.

Misc.: 1/4" dia. plugs (8); 1/4" dia. peg (1); 1/2" dia. plugs (2); 1-1/4" and 1-1/2" finishing nails; no. 8 x 1-1/4" FHWS; 5/16" I.D. washers (10); 1/4" dia. x 2" dowel; 1/2" thick x 1-1/2" dia. wheel.

RUGGED RIG

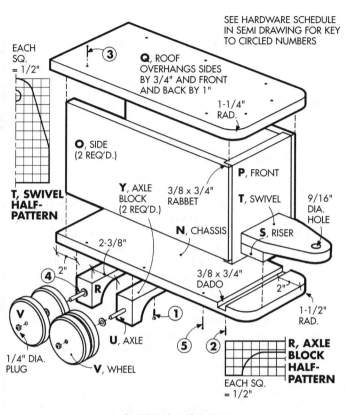

EACH SQ. = 1/2"

T, SWIVEL HALF-PATTERN

Q, ROOF OVERHANGS SIDES BY 3/4" AND FRONT AND BACK BY 1"

SEE HARDWARE SCHEDULE IN SEMI DRAWING FOR KEY TO CIRCLED NUMBERS

1-1/4" RAD.

O, SIDE (2 REQ'D.)

P, FRONT

Y, AXLE BLOCK (2 REQ'D.) 3/8 x 3/4" RABBET

T, SWIVEL

9/16" DIA. HOLE

N, CHASSIS

S, RISER

2-3/8"

3/8 x 3/4" DADO

2"

1-1/2" RAD.

U, AXLE

R

V

1/4" DIA. PLUG

V, WHEEL

R, AXLE BLOCK HALF-PATTERN

EACH SQ. = 1/2"

CUTTING LIST: VAN
(all parts pine except where noted)

Key	No.	Part, Mat'l.	Size
N	1	Chassis	3/4 x 7 x 18"
O	2	Sides	3/4 x 7 x 15"
P	1	Front	3/4 x 6-1/4 x 7-3/8"
Q	1	Roof	3/4 x 8-1/2 x 17"
R	2	Axle blocks, Maple	1-1/2 x 2 x 7"
S	1	Riser	3/4 x 2 x 4"
T	1	Swivel	3/4 x 4 x 6"
U	2	Axles, Dowel	5/16" dia. x 10"
V	8	Wheels, Hard wood or particleboard	3/4" x 3-1/2" dia.

Misc.: 1/4" dia. plugs (4); 1-1/2" and 2" finishing nails; 5/16" I.D. washers (8).

To complete the cab assembly, cut the roof **G** to size and round the edges using a router with a 1/4-in. rounding over bit (or use sandpaper wrapped around a sanding block). Attach the roof with glue and drive one nail in each corner. The back of the roof is flush with the back of the cab.

FRONT END

Form the engine **H** from a solid block or by gluing together four pieces of 3/4-in.-thick pine. Cut the part to size; then shape the corners with a router or a belt sander. Next, bore holes for the plugs that act as the hood ornament and the headlights; then glue and clamp the engine to the chassis and cab front. Now glue in the steering wheel assembly, which is made from a store-bought wheel and a piece of dowel. Cut the bumper **I** and glue and nail it to the front of the chassis. Don't forget

lay out the seat **F** on a 2x4; then cut it out using a band saw. Round the front corner of the seat using a router with a 3/8-in. rounding over bit, or you can simply sand it by hand. Install the seat with glue.

MAKING WHEELS FOR THE SEMI AND VAN

Although many catalogs supply ready-to-use wheels in various sizes and designs, you can make your own wheels with a few simple tools and jigs.

An adjustable wheel and circle cutter — also known as a fly cutter — can be used in a drill press to make the wheels for the semi and the van. A small circle cutter can cut wheels from 7/8 to 4 in. dia. The cutter's center pilot perfectly centers the axle hole.

USING THE FLY CUTTER

The cutter must be used at a very slow speed in a drill press. Use a backup board beneath the workpiece so the cutter does not scrape the drill press table. Clamp both the backup board and the workpiece securely to the table. Feed the cutter slowly into the workpiece and keep your hands far from the cutter. You may want to paint the top edge of the cutter and the beam that connects the cutter to the body to make them more visible.

Once you've cut the wheels, chamfer the edges. This can be done on a stationary belt sander with a wheel-chamfering jig made from scraps (see drawing and photo below right). The dowel that holds the wheel should fit tight and should be glued into the pivot. It should also be long enough to pass through the pivot so it abuts the angled side, acting as a stop. To use the jig, clamp it to the sander table and place a wheel on the dowel. Move the pivot until the wheel contacts the moving belt and chamfers the perimeter of the wheel. Swing the pivot away, turn the wheel over and chamfer the other side.

to bore the holes for the two plugs in the bumper.

Cut the fenders J with a band saw or a table saw. Enlarge the fender pattern (see drawing) on a photocopier or draw a grid of 1/2-in. squares directly onto a piece of pine. Then mark the pattern on your workpiece and cut it out. Whatever method you use, sand the saw marks and round the outside edges. Attach the fenders with glue and nails.

Make the wheels next using a fly cutter. Cut the axles to length and slide them into the holes in the axle blocks. The wheels should fit snugly on the axles, so be sure the dowels you use are the right size. Glue the wheels to the axles, adding washers between the double wheels and between the wheels and axle blocks; then glue in the wood plugs. Finally, bore a hole for the 1/2-in.-dia. dowel pin in the riser B. The pin is used to hook up the van.

Finish the truck with two coats of polyurethane varnish and decorate it with various kinds of adhesive tape.

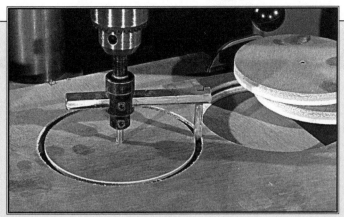

When using a fly cutter to make wheels, operate your drill press at the slowest speed. The cutter is shown making plywood wheels.

WHEEL CHAMFERING JIG

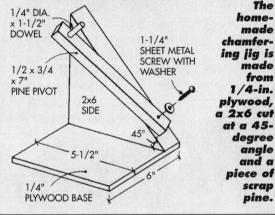

1/4" DIA. x 1-1/2" DOWEL

1/2 x 3/4 x 7" PINE PIVOT

2x6 SIDE

1-1/4" SHEET METAL SCREW WITH WASHER

45°

5-1/2"

6"

1/4" PLYWOOD BASE

The home-made chamfering jig is made from 1/4-in. plywood, a 2x6 cut at a 45-degree angle and a piece of scrap pine.

BUILDING THE VAN

The van is similar to the semi in many respects. In fact, the general construction techniques — including the use of a dado in the chassis, the installation of the top, the shape of the axle blocks and the size and installation of the wheels — are identical. The following instructions guide you through the order of construction. Refer back to the text about the construction of the semi for specifics.

Cut the chassis **N** to size. Next, cut the dadoes for the front **P**; then round the front corners of the chassis. Cut the sides **O**; then cut the rabbets with a router and 3/4-in. straight bit. Glue and nail the sides to the front; then attach the assembly to the chassis.

Add the roof **Q**; then cut and install the axle blocks **R**. The only difference between these axle blocks and the ones installed on the semi is the length.

Assemble the riser **S** and swivel **T** as a unit; then glue and nail the assembly to the chassis. Cut the axles **U** and install the wheels **V**.

STACK-AND-ROLL

his 12-wheel pull toy is flexible, so the wheels can be stacked up in a variety of arrangements. The action is absorbing enough that this could be an adult's desktop toy. And if you don't mind looking ridiculous, it makes a great back massager — simply lie down on the toy so that your spine is between the two rows of wheels and have someone you trust roll you back and forth.

You can easily reproduce the toy with basic tools. The toy shown is made of maple and walnut, but just about any wood will do. You'll need 1 board ft. of 1x stock (3/4 in. actual size) and 3 ft. of 3/8-in.-dia. dowel. The toy is easier to build if you use a table saw, a drill press and a belt sander, but you could use hand tools. You'll need a 2-1/4-in. hole saw with a removable pilot bit to make the wheels.

CUTTING THE WHEELS

Select enough wood to make 12 2-1/4-in.-dia. wheels **A** and sand the surface before

The pull toy is composed of 12 wheels and 10 spacers held together with dowels. When the wheels are stacked, they spin in opposite directions, creating a striking visual effect.

PULL TOY

you begin to cut. It saves time to bore the 3/8-in.-dia. axle holes when you cut the wheels with the hole saw, but most hole saw bits are 1/4 in. dia. To solve this problem, you can cut off the 1/4-in. shank of a 3/8-in. spade bit so it is about 1 in. long and replace the original bit with the spade bit. You'll need to grind a flat spot on the shank to seat the mandrel set screw.

The toy works only if the axles fit snugly in the axle holes, so test the fit of the dowel in a hole before you drill the rest of the holes. You may need to buy larger dowels.

Position the wheel stock in the drill press (photo 1, p. 46) and cut most of the way through; then turn the stock over and complete the cut from the other side.

After you've cut all the wheels, remove saw marks and burn marks with a belt sander. To sand six wheels at once, slip them onto a 1/4-in.-dia. rod with

a washer on each end (photo 2).

SPACERS AND AXLES

To make the spacers **B,C,D**, rip 1x hard wood to 3/4 x 3/4 in. For contrast, four of the spacers on the toy shown were made out of walnut; the others were made out of maple. Sand the sides and edges of the stock; then cut the spacers to length. The length shown in the cutting list on p. 47

1 When you cut the wheels, position the stock so that the hole saw just breaks through an edge. This allows the sawdust to escape, so the hole saw cuts much faster and stays cooler.

3 Clamp a fence with a stop on your drill press to position the spacers. The distance between the center of the holes should equal the wheel diameter.

2 Sand the wheels at an angle so they turn slowly. Flip the rod end over end and repeat. A large washer on each end protects your fingers.

4 To avoid sticky fingers when applying finish to the spacers and wheels, insert dowels in the axle holes to hold the parts.

(3-5/8 in.) is correct for 2-1/4-in.-dia. wheels. (The spacers should be 1-3/8 in. longer than the diameter of the wheels.)

Now drill 1/2-in.-dia. through-holes for the axles in the spacers (photo 3). Drill a 1/2-in.-dia. hole 3/8 in. deep perpendicular to the axle hole in the front center spacer **C** (see Front Center Spacer Detail). Bore the rest of the way through with a 3/16-

in. bit. You'll attach the pull string here later. Bevel the edges of all the spacers with sandpaper.

Next, cut six axles **E** from 3/8-in.-dia. dowel. To determine the axle length, calculate the total thickness of the two wheels and three spacers and add 1/8 in. Sand any remaining rough surfaces and edges and clean up all of the holes by countersinking them slightly. Bevel the axle ends by twist-

STACK-AND-ROLL PULL TOY

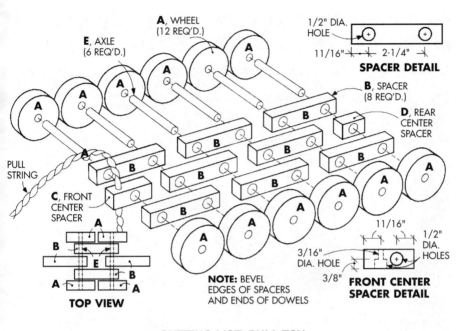

A, WHEEL (12 REQ'D.)

E, AXLE (6 REQ'D.)

1/2" DIA. HOLE

11/16" — 2-1/4"

SPACER DETAIL

B, SPACER (8 REQ'D.)

D, REAR CENTER SPACER

PULL STRING

C, FRONT CENTER SPACER

11/16"

3/16" DIA. HOLE

1/2" DIA. HOLES

3/8"

FRONT CENTER SPACER DETAIL

TOP VIEW

NOTE: BEVEL EDGES OF SPACERS AND ENDS OF DOWELS

CUTTING LIST: PULL TOY

Key	No.	Part, Mat'l.	Size	Key	No.	Part, Mat'l.	Size
A	12	Wheels, Maple	3/4 x 2-1/4" dia.	D	1	Rear center spacer, Maple	3/4 x 3/4 x 1-3/8"
B	8	Spacers, Maple, walnut (4 ea.)	3/4 x 3/4 x 3-5/8"	E	6	Axles, Dowel	3/8" dia. x 3-7/8"
C	1	Front center spacer, Maple	3/4 x 3/4 x 2"				

Misc.: Pull string (30").

ing them on a belt sander.

FINISHING AND ASSEMBLY

All finishing should be done before you assemble the toy. Use artist's acrylics to paint the yin yang designs on the wheels. When the paint is dry, apply two coats of clear finish to the wheels and spacers (photo 4). Spray on lacquer or brush on polyurethane. Prop the parts on dowels to dry.

Don't apply finish to the axles. Instead, rub them with paraffin or beeswax to serve as axle grease. Leave the ends bare where the axles will be

glued into the wheels.

Coat one end of each axle with yellow carpenter's glue and tap it into a wheel. Slip on the spacers and glue the remaining six wheels onto the other ends of the axles.

Now find a string about 30 in. long that can be used to pull the toy. Tie a large knot at one end of the string and pull the other end through the pull-string hole so that the knot rests in the large end of the hole. Your toy is ready to pull and play — or to soothe your tired back muscles.

BUILDING BLOCKS

With a good set of building blocks, imaginative children can build formidable castles, intricate bridges and majestic skyscrapers. By making simple variations on a standard block (see drawing), you can create myriad shapes and sizes that inspire architectural wonders. The blocks are easily stored in a simple plywood box (inset).

With a little planning, you can make a set of building blocks that readily lends itself to architectural masterpieces. The key is to make all the dimensions multiples of one basic measurement: the stock thickness.

Consider a basic building block — twice as wide and four times as long as it is thick. The set you see here is made from 1-1/2-in.-thick stock, so the basic shape is 1-1/2 x 3 x 6 in. Now think of all the ways you can divide and multiply this shape. You can probably come up with even more possibilities than are shown in the drawing below.

CHAMFER ALL EDGES 1/8"

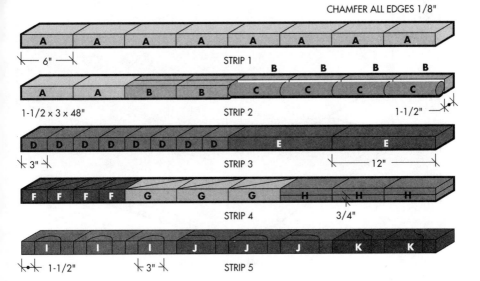

STRIP 1
6"

STRIP 2
1-1/2 x 3 x 48"   1-1/2"

STRIP 3
3"   12"

STRIP 4
3/4"

STRIP 5
1-1/2"   3"

STORAGE BOX

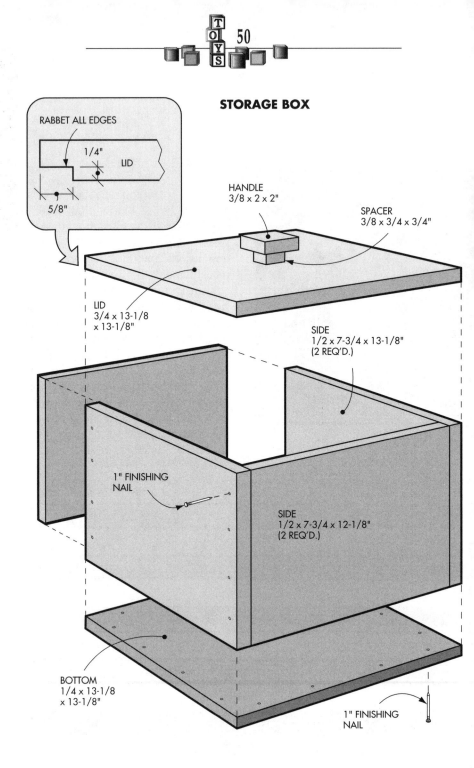

RABBET ALL EDGES

1/4"

LID

5/8"

HANDLE
3/8 x 2 x 2"

SPACER
3/8 x 3/4 x 3/4"

LID
3/4 x 13-1/8
x 13-1/8"

SIDE
1/2 x 7-3/4 x 13-1/8"
(2 REQ'D.)

1" FINISHING
NAIL

SIDE
1/2 x 7-3/4 x 12-1/8"
(2 REQ'D.)

BOTTOM
1/4 x 13-1/8
x 13-1/8"

1" FINISHING
NAIL

BUILDING BLOCKS

The blocks shown were made from 1-1/2-in. maple butcher block (5 sq. ft. not counting waste). You can often buy scraps of butcher block from shops that make cabinets or countertops, or you can substitute pine 2x4s or 1-1/2-in.-thick poplar.

Begin by ripping 15-1/2 ft. of 1-1/2- x 3-in. stock, 6 ft. of 1-1/2- x 1-1/2-in. stock and 3 ft. of 3/4- x 3-in. stock, allowing a little extra for waste. Use a band saw or a table saw with a good 10-in. ripping blade.

After you've ripped the stock to width and cut it to the proper thickness, cut 1/8-in. chamfers on all edges using a router with a 45-degree chamfering bit. Sand the sides of the boards before you begin to cut individual blocks.

Note that the curves in blocks I,J and K are 1-1/2-in. radius. (This large scale is a good idea because the blocks are too big to fit into the mouths of very young architects.) You can use a compass to draw the curves, or you can enlarge the grid patterns to full size using a photocopier or draw them on graph paper with 1-in. squares and then trace the patterns onto the stock. Cut the curves with a band saw and sand the insides with a 2-in. drum sander on a drill press.

If you don't want to turn the round pillars (blocks **C**) on a lathe, you can simply buy a 1-1/2-in.-dia. dowel (curtain rod) and cut it into 6-in. lengths.

After you've cut all the blocks to their finished sizes and shapes, chamfer the remaining edges and sand them smooth. Now you're ready to apply a finish. Just about any finish will do — you can use oil, varnish, lacquer or paint. All 68 of the blocks fit in an 8- x 13-1/8- x 13-1/8-in. box made of plywood (see drawing, opposite page). The box sides are joined with glue and 1-in. finishing nails.

EACH SQ = 1"

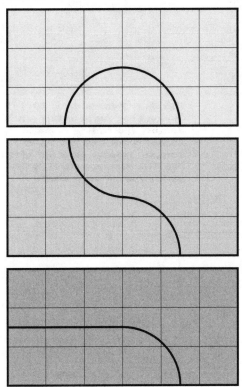

BLOCK PATTERNS

TOY TUGBOAT

This 3-1/2-in.-wide x 10-1/2-in.-long toy tugboat has realistic details: The railing is made from basket reed, and the radar antenna rotates on a pin mounting. The boat can float in the bathtub or sit on a shelf.

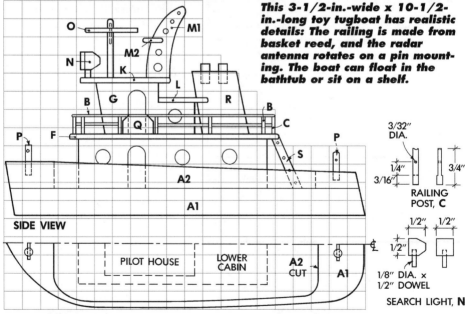

SIDE VIEW

HULL—HALF PATTERN

PILOT HOUSE

LOWER CABIN

A2 CUT

A1

3/32" DIA.

1/4"

3/16"

3/4"

RAILING POST, **C**

1/2"

1/2"

1/2"

1/8" DIA. x 1/2" DOWEL

SEARCH LIGHT, **N**

TOY TUGBOAT

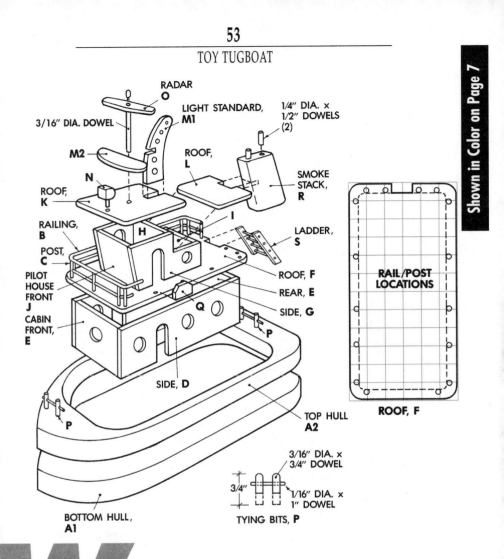

RADAR
O

3/16" DIA. DOWEL

LIGHT STANDARD, M1

1/4" DIA. x 1/2" DOWELS (2)

M2

N

ROOF, K

RAILING, B

POST, C

PILOT HOUSE FRONT J

CABIN FRONT, E

ROOF, L

H

I

SMOKE STACK, R

LADDER, S

ROOF, F

REAR, E

SIDE, G

Q

P

SIDE, D

P

TOP HULL A2

RAIL/POST LOCATIONS

ROOF, F

BOTTOM HULL, A1

3/16" DIA. x 3/4" DOWEL

3/4"

1/16" DIA. x 1" DOWEL

TYING BITS, P

With their stubby bows straining against the hulls of the ships that dwarf them, even real tugboats seem like toys. This miniature version looks and floats like the real McCoy.

All the parts are made of pine except for the railing, which is made of 2.25mm basket reed (available at craft-supply stores). If you paint the boat, apply the paint as you make the assemblies but before you glue them to the hull.

HULL AND CABINS

Using the pattern on the opposite page, make a half-template of the hull. Then cut two blocks, one for the bottom hull **A1** and one for the top hull **A2**. Temporarily nail the two halves together with three 1-in. finishing nails. Offset the two pieces so that the top hull is 1/8 in. in front of the bottom hull.

Use a belt or disc sander to shape the hull. Sand the sides so they gently

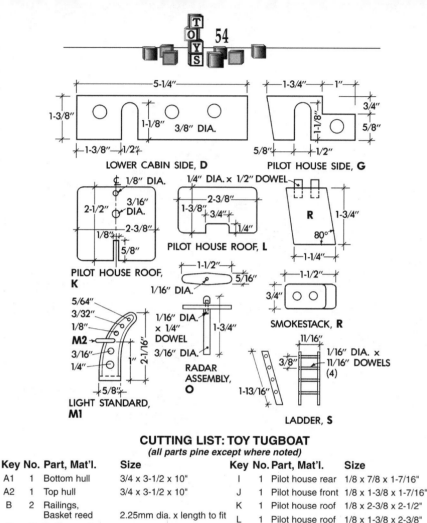

LOWER CABIN SIDE, **D**

PILOT HOUSE SIDE, **G**

PILOT HOUSE ROOF, **L**

PILOT HOUSE ROOF, **K**

SMOKESTACK, **R**

RADAR ASSEMBLY, **O**

LIGHT STANDARD, **M1**

LADDER, **S**

CUTTING LIST: TOY TUGBOAT
(all parts pine except where noted)

Key	No.	Part, Mat'l.	Size	Key	No.	Part, Mat'l.	Size
A1	1	Bottom hull	3/4 x 3-1/2 x 10"	I	1	Pilot house rear	1/8 x 7/8 x 1-7/16"
A2	1	Top hull	3/4 x 3-1/2 x 10"	J	1	Pilot house front	1/8 x 1-3/8 x 1-7/16"
B	2	Railings, Basket reed	2.25mm dia. x length to fit	K	1	Pilot house roof	1/8 x 2-3/8 x 2-1/2"
				L	1	Pilot house roof	1/8 x 1-3/8 x 2-3/8"
C	17	Railing posts, Dowel	1/8" dia. x 3/4"	M1	1	Light standard	1/8 x 1-1/4 x 2-1/16"
D	2	Lower cabin sides	3/16 x 1-3/8 x 5-1/4"	M2	1	Light standard	1/8 x 1/2 x 1-1/4"
				N	1	Searchlight	1/2 x 1/2 x 1/2"
E	2	Front/rear lower cabin	3/16 x 1-3/8 x 1-7/8"	O	1	Radar assembly	1/8 x 1/4 x 1-3/4"
				P	4	Tying bits, Dowel	3/16" dia. x 3/4"
F	1	Lower cabin roof	5/32 x 3 x 6"	Q	2	Logo plate	1/16 x 11/16 x 15/16"
G	2	Pilot house sides	1/8 x 1-3/8 x 2-3/4"	R	1	Smokestack	3/4 x 1-1/2 x 1-3/4"
H	1	Pilot house center	1/8 x 1-3/8 x 1-7/16"	S	2	Ladder	3/32 x 1/4 x 1-13/16"

Misc.: 1/16" dia. dowel for ladder and tying bits; white or yellow glue.

slope toward the front, ending with a 10-degree slope on the bow. Turn the hull over and sand the stern to a 10-degree slope.

Separate the two sections and, with the same template, mark the cutout in the top hull. Drill an entry hole in the top hull and carefully make the cutout with a scroll saw. Keep the waste piece — you'll use it later as a jig when you make the railing.

Mark a downward sloping line

TOY TUGBOAT

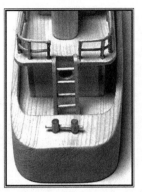

from the front to the rear on the top hull (see the side view drawing, p. 52). Sand along this line, but be sure to leave a slight hump in the center of the rear deck (photo, right). Now glue both sections of the hull together.

RAILING AND CABINS

Soon you'll need the cutout from the top hull section to use as a jig to form the basket-reed railings **B**. First, soak the reed in warm water for two or three hours or until it's pliable.

Meanwhile, make the railing posts **C** from 1/8-in. dowel. Use a sharp knife to trim the sides flat (leave the dowel bottom round to fit into the cabin roof holes); then bore a 3/32-in. hole to pass the lower railing through. Cut a V-notch on the top of each post for the upper rail.

When the reed has become pliable, wipe off the excess water and tack one end of the reed to the narrow end of the jig; then wrap the reed tightly around the jig perimeter three or four times. Tack the other end of the reed next to the starting place and let it dry overnight. You need only two railings, but it pays to have extra.

Rip stock for the lower cabin **D,E** and roof **F**; then cut the parts to size. The exact thickness isn't critical — if you're off, adjust the size of the pieces so the outside dimensions of the cabin are the same as in the drawing. Drill the portholes and cut the doors. Assemble the sides (but not the roof) and glue them to the hull.

Leave a slight hump in the stern to add realism. Cut the angles on the ladder before installation.

RAILING

Use the roof pattern p. 53, to locate post holes in the roof **F** and bore them with a 1/8-in. brad-point drill bit. After boring the holes, cut the notch for the ladder.

Thread the dry basket reed through the holes in the railing posts. When all are threaded, insert the posts in the holes. To attach the top railing, use a hot-melt glue gun to place a small drop of glue on the V-notch starting at the front center and working along each side until you reach the ladder end. Trim the reed flush with the posts that meet the ladder.

Construct the pilot house (parts **G** through **L**) from 1/8-in. stock, or use the same 3/16-in. stock as the lower cabin but adjust the size so the outside dimensions of the pilot house match the drawing dimension. Cut the doors and drill portholes before assembling. Make the necessary notch for the light standard **M1,M2**, and bore holes for the searchlight **N** and radar assembly **O**.

Bore the holes in the hull for the tying bits **P**; then make the other detail pieces — the logo plate **Q**, the smokestack **R** and the ladder **S** — and glue them in place.

Finally, apply several coats of a spray polyurethane varnish or an oil-base enamel to protect the boat from rough bathtub waves.

TOY TRAIN

Always a favorite with kids, this basic wooden train is about 35 in. long but can be made longer if you build duplicate cars or design new ones.

Pardon me boy, is that the Chattanooga Choo Choo? The youngsters who play with this train set probably haven't heard that old melody, but you can whistle it as you build.

This simple project is made easier if you order hard-to-make parts such as

the smokestack, wheels, axle pegs, and passengers from Cherry Tree Toys Inc. (Box 369, Belmont, OH 43718; 800-848-4363), but patterns are provided in the drawing if you want to turn these parts on a lathe. You can make the remainder of the components with a table saw or band saw. A palm sander is helpful for shaping the curves on some parts, and a drill press is best for drilling accurate axle holes.

PREPARING STOCK

This is a good project for making use of scraps left over from bigger projects, so you might want to make it from a hodgepodge of different kinds of wood you have around the shop. If you don't have a lot of scraps, make it out of construction-grade pine and cut around the knots. You'll need a 1x12 (3/4 x 11-1/4 in. actual size) about 4 or 5 ft. long, depending on how many knots are in the board.

There are a lot of different part sizes, so the best way to deal with your stock is to group parts of the same thickness and make them from a single piece. You'll need a 2-1/4-in.-wide x 24-in. length of 3/4-in. stock; a 2-3/4-in.-wide x 60-in. length of 5/8-in. stock and a 2-3/4-in.-wide x 48-in. length of 1/4-in. stock (or use a band

Shown in Color on Page 6

1 To resaw or cut stock to thickness on the table saw, use a rip or combination blade (shown). A pushstick allows you to keep your fingers clear of the saw blade.

2 A smooth plane is an effective way to quickly remove saw marks. No sanding is required after planing. The thickness of the pieces isn't critical, but they should be flat to ensure a good glue bond. Use a bench stop to prevent the work from sliding.

3 When crosscutting long stock to make parts, set the saw blade so the teeth protrude just above the top of the stock. You'll get a smooth and safe cut. An auxiliary fence screwed to the miter gauge lets you hold the stock with your hand away from the blade.

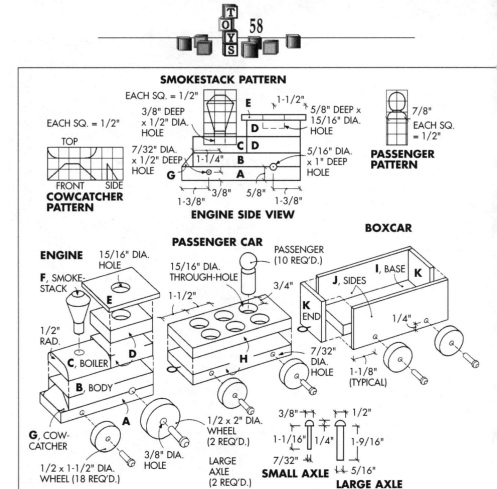

SMOKESTACK PATTERN

EACH SQ. = 1/2"

3/8" DEEP x 1/2" DIA. HOLE

E

D

1-1/2"

5/8" DEEP x 15/16" DIA. HOLE

7/8"

PASSENGER PATTERN

EACH SQ. = 1/2"

EACH SQ. = 1/2"

TOP

7/32" DIA. x 1/2" DEEP HOLE

FRONT **SIDE**

COWCATCHER PATTERN

C **D**

1-1/4" **B**

G **A**

3/8" 5/8"

1-3/8"

5/16" DIA. x 1" DEEP HOLE

ENGINE SIDE VIEW

3/8" 1-3/8"

BOXCAR

PASSENGER CAR

PASSENGER (10 REQ'D.)

I, BASE **K**

ENGINE 15/16" DIA. HOLE

15/16" DIA. THROUGH-HOLE

3/4"

J, SIDES

F, SMOKE-STACK

E

1-1/2"

K END

K END

1/4"

1/2" RAD.

C, BOILER

D

H

7/32" DIA. HOLE

1-1/8" (TYPICAL)

B, BODY

A

1/2 x 2" DIA. WHEEL (2 REQ'D.)

3/8" 1/2"

G, COW-CATCHER

3/8" DIA. HOLE

1-1/16" 1/4" 1-9/16"

1/2 x 1-1/2" DIA. WHEEL (18 REQ'D.)

LARGE AXLE (2 REQ'D.)

7/32"

SMALL AXLE 5/16"

LARGE AXLE

4 *Use a 1-in. belt sander to shape the cowcatcher. Make light passes to prevent the sanding belt from grabbing and throwing the workpiece. If you don't have a bench-top sander, clamp a hand-held belt sander upside down to your workbench to shape the cowcatcher.*

saw or table saw to resaw a 24-in. piece of 3/4-in. stock in half). Of course, you'll cut these pieces to the sizes required for the smaller parts. But for now, keep the pieces as long as possible. (It's safer to work with longer stock and easier to deal with fewer parts.)

Once you've cut the pieces to length, mill the 1/4- and 5/8-in. stock to the correct thick-

TOY TRAIN

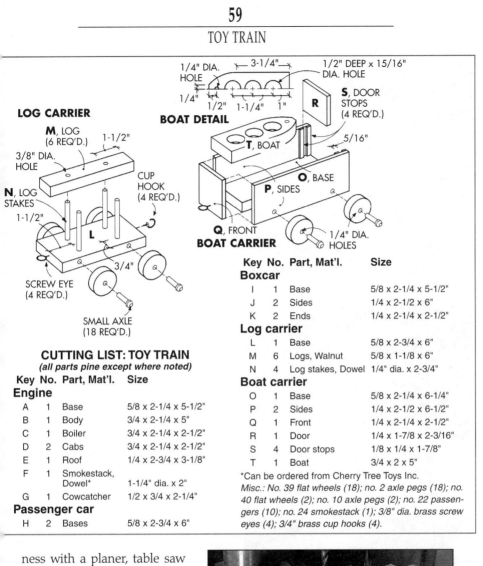

LOG CARRIER

BOAT DETAIL

1/4" DIA. HOLE

3-1/4"

1/2" DEEP x 15/16" DIA. HOLE

S, DOOR STOPS (4 REQ'D.)

R

T, BOAT

5/16"

O, BASE

P, SIDES

M, LOG (6 REQ'D.)

1-1/2"

3/8" DIA. HOLE

CUP HOOK (4 REQ'D.)

N, LOG STAKES

1-1/2"

L

3/4"

SCREW EYE (4 REQ'D.)

SMALL AXLE (18 REQ'D.)

Q, FRONT

BOAT CARRIER

1/4" DIA. HOLES

CUTTING LIST: TOY TRAIN
(all parts pine except where noted)

Key	No.	Part, Mat'l.	Size
Engine			
A	1	Base	5/8 x 2-1/4 x 5-1/2"
B	1	Body	3/4 x 2-1/4 x 5"
C	1	Boiler	3/4 x 2-1/4 x 2-1/2"
D	2	Cabs	3/4 x 2-1/4 x 2-1/2"
E	1	Roof	1/4 x 2-3/4 x 3-1/8"
F	1	Smokestack, Dowel*	1-1/4" dia. x 2"
G	1	Cowcatcher	1/2 x 3/4 x 2-1/4"
Passenger car			
H	2	Bases	5/8 x 2-3/4 x 6"

Key	No.	Part, Mat'l.	Size
Boxcar			
I	1	Base	5/8 x 2-1/4 x 5-1/2"
J	2	Sides	1/4 x 2-1/2 x 6"
K	2	Ends	1/4 x 2-1/4 x 2-1/2"
Log carrier			
L	1	Base	5/8 x 2-3/4 x 6"
M	6	Logs, Walnut	5/8 x 1-1/8 x 6"
N	4	Log stakes, Dowel	1/4" dia. x 2-3/4"
Boat carrier			
O	1	Base	5/8 x 2-1/4 x 6-1/4"
P	2	Sides	1/4 x 2-1/2 x 6-1/2"
Q	1	Front	1/4 x 2-1/4 x 2-1/2"
R	1	Door	1/4 x 1-7/8 x 2-3/16"
S	4	Door stops	1/8 x 1/4 x 1-7/8"
T	1	Boat	3/4 x 2 x 5"

*Can be ordered from Cherry Tree Toys Inc.
Misc.: No. 39 flat wheels (18); no. 2 axle pegs (18); no. 40 flat wheels (2); no. 10 axle pegs (2); no. 22 passengers (10); no. 24 smokestack (1); 3/8" dia. brass screw eyes (4); 3/4" brass cup hooks (4).

ness with a planer, table saw or band saw. To do this using a table saw, first set the fence at just a hair over the thickness you want; then run the stock through on edge. You'll sand off the extra stock later.

To be safe, set the blade height at just over half the total width of the parts that are to be cut to thickness. Push the parts through on

5 *Use a fence and stop block clamped to the drill press table to ensure consistent results when boring holes in the logs M (shown) and for boring axle holes. If you don't have a drill press, use a portable drill guide to hold the work in a vise.*

6 A fence is also helpful when drilling holes for the passengers — in this case the engineer's position. Hold the work firmly to prevent it from spinning.

7 If the smokestack fits too loosely in the engine, wrap shavings from a plane around the bottom and glue them in place.

8 Apply glue only in the axle holes, not to the pegs; otherwise glue is likely to be forced between the axle pegs and the wheels and keep them from turning.

one edge; then flip the parts to complete the cut (photo 1, p. 57). Be sure to use a pushstick. You can use the same procedure to resaw 3/4-in. stock to get two 1/4-in. pieces. After sawing, smooth the pieces with a hand plane (photo 2), or use a belt sander or palm sander.

Now you can rip parts to width and then to length. (It's much safer and more efficient to work in this order.) To get the most out of the stock, look over the cutting list again; then group together parts of the same thickness and width.

MAKING PARTS

For safety and speed, use the table saw jigs shown in photo 3 to cut parts to length. (If you use a radial arm saw to cut the pieces, you should use a pushstick to hold the work and be sure to keep your fingers clear of the blade.) Screw an auxiliary fence to the miter gauge that's long enough to support the parts on both sides of the cut. Clamp a 1-in.-wide piece of scrap to the saw fence several inches in front of the blade and use this piece as the stop for determining part lengths. The space between this piece and the fence prevents the work from becoming trapped between the blade and the fence — a dangerous situation that can cause the work to be thrown by the blade.

To cut a part, first place it against the auxiliary miter fence, well in front of the blade. Butt the end of the part against the scrap piece that's clamped to the saw fence. Hold the part securely against the miter fence so that it doesn't move; then push it through the blade.

Round over the two sides of the engine boiler **C** with a small block plane or 1-in. belt sander. Carefully shape the cowcatcher **G** (photo 4, p. 58) using the squared patterns in the drawing.

ASSEMBLING PARTS

An easy way to glue the engine parts together is to use the front edge of your workbench to back up the work. When you clamp, there will be less of a tendency for the pieces to slide out of alignment. The best way to clamp the cowcatcher is to tightly pull masking tape around the front of the catcher, attaching the tape to the engine body **B**.

Gluing together the boxcar and boat carrier is a bit tricky because you have a lot of small parts to assemble at once. When clamping, use wooden clamp pads to avoid crushing the parts. For the passenger car, glue the two 5/8- x 2-3/4- x 6-in. pieces together, but bore the passenger holes in the top piece first.

For accuracy, use a drill press to bore all holes. Employ a drill press setup like the one shown in photo 5 to bore accurate holes in the logs **M**. Clamp a fence to the drill press table to locate the drill bit in the center of the logs and a stop block to locate the holes from the ends. Use a similar setup to bore holes in the log-carrier car for the vertical posts.

Next, bore the axle holes. Use a tall fence to support the cars while they are on edge. You'll need to switch the stop block from one side to the other to bore some of the axle holes. Before boring the engine axle holes, put a spacer under the engine to prevent the cab roof from tilting the engine.

Use a 15/16-in. spade bit to bore holes for the passengers in the boat **T**, passenger car and engine (photo 6). Note that the spade bit's spur will penetrate the bottom of the boat, which can cause it to sink. Prevent this nautical disaster by boring these holes to a plug size and then gluing in plugs. If you have a 15/16-in. Forstner bit, use it to bore these holes. Forstner bits don't have center spurs, so you won't have this problem.

While you're set up at the drill press to bore the seat for the engineer, bore the hole for the smokestack, too. If the smokestack fits loosely in the hole, use the technique shown in photo 7 for a better fit.

It's easiest to finish the cars before you put on the wheels. Roll small pieces of paper and stuff them into the axle holes so the finish won't get in and prevent a good glue bond. A quick way to finish the cars is to use spray shellac, which is available at hardware stores. Shellac dries quickly and provides a tough finish. However, if the boat is going to end up in the bathtub, use an exterior-grade varnish, not shellac. Whatever finish you use, provide good cross-ventilation.

To attach the wheels, first apply glue in the car and engine axle holes (photo 8); then twist the axle into the hole to spread the glue evenly.

All that remains is to get some hooks and screw eyes at the hardware store, screw them in place and start selling tickets to Chattanooga!

UP PERISCOPE

A periscope is a great toy for kids, but some adults will appreciate its practical applications: For instance, sports fans can use it for a better view at crowded games.

Beginning woodworkers should have a field day making this periscope. It is a fairly easy project to build, and it appeals to kids and adults.

The periscope is not much more than a box made from 3/8-in.-thick pine with small mirror pieces added. You may be able to find a 3/8-in. casing at a lumberyard or home center; then you'd only have to rip the pieces to width with a sabre saw, band saw or table saw. When you rip the casing, you'll remove the shaped edges

UP PERISCOPE

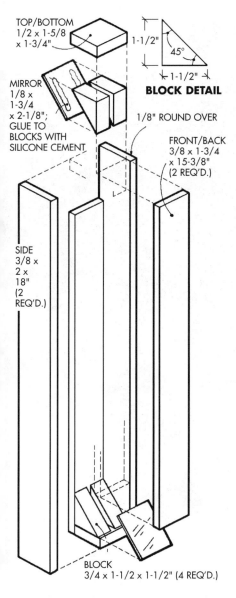

TOP/BOTTOM
1/2 x 1-5/8
x 1-3/4"

1-1/2"

45°

1-1/2"

BLOCK DETAIL

MIRROR
1/8 x
1-3/4
x 2-1/8";
GLUE TO
BLOCKS WITH
SILICONE CEMENT

1/8" ROUND OVER

FRONT/BACK
3/8 x 1-3/4
x 15-3/8"
(2 REQ'D.)

SIDE
3/8 x
2 x
18"
(2
REQ'D.)

BLOCK
3/4 x 1-1/2 x 1-1/2" (4 REQ'D.)

PRODUCTION-STYLE TECHNIQUES

If you're making more than one periscope, save yourself time by working production style. Just figure out how many pieces you'll need and rip enough 1-3/4- and 2-in. pieces at once. Crosscut all the parts to length next with a sabre saw or radial arm saw. Crosscut the top and bottom pieces as well.

You should now be ready to glue the sides to the front and back. To avoid confusion during gluing, mark the insides of the sides in pencil where the front and back pieces go: One is flush with the top of the sides; the other is flush with the bottom. Use a glue bottle with a small nozzle and squeeze a small bead on the edges of the front and back pieces. Spread the glue evenly with your finger; then clamp gently with C-clamps. Use protective blocks between the clamp pads and the periscope parts to avoid damage.

If the joints appear tight, it's not necessary to nail the parts together. If you don't have clamps, use nails to keep the joints tight until the glue dries. The nails should be small — 3/4-in. brads — and driven straight.

Glue in the top and bottom pieces; then cut the triangular blocks from 3/4-in. pine. Glue the blocks in place.

FINISHING TOUCHES

Sand all of the parts with 150-grit sandpaper; then apply a spray polyurethane varnish or paint. After the finish has dried, all that's left is to add the mirror or mirrored acrylic for the final touch. Glue it to the blocks with silicone cement.

and be left with square edges for easy joining. If you can't buy 3/8-in. stock, you can make the periscope out of 1/4- or 3/8-in.-thick lattice strips.

TIC-TAC-TOE

eginners can make this tic-tac-toe box using only a handsaw and a drill. More experienced woodworkers can crank out several in a day working production style with a table saw and a drill press.

To start the project you need a piece of 1/2- x 6-in. pine about 9 in. long for the top and drawer sides. The box sides and back are cut from 3/4-in. pine. The box bottom and the drawer bottom are made of 1/4-in. plywood.

Make the box parts by placing a 3/4-in. pine strip in a miter box. Cut as

TIC-TAC-TOE

This tic-tac-toe board is easy to make — all you need is a handsaw and a drill.

1/16" DEEP x 1/8" WIDE GROOVES

TOP, 1/2 x 5 x 5"

1/4"

3/8"

3/16" DEEP x 1/2" DIA. HOLE

BACK 3/4 x 1-1/2 x 5"

45° MITER

BOTTOM, 1/4 x 4-1/4 x 4-5/8" PLYWOOD

SIDE 3/4 x 1-1/4 x 5" (2 REQ'D.)

1-1/2" 1/2"

SIDE, 1/2 x 1 x 4-1/4" (2 REQ'D.)

FRONT/BACK 1/2 x 1 x 3-1/2"

BOTTOM, 1/4 x 3 x 3-3/4" PLYWOOD

1/4 x 1/4" RABBET

3/4" BRAD

DRAWER

shown in the drawing. If you have a router or table saw, cut the rabbet in the sides; then cut and nail in the bottom. If you don't have these power tools, cut the bottom 5 x 5 in. instead of using the dimensions shown, and nail the bottom to the sides flush with the outside of the box parts.

Cut the top to size next; then lay out the grooves that delineate the tic-tac-toe boxes with a ruler and pencil. Cut the grooves on a table saw or use a handsaw. Bore the holes where the marbles rest. A Forstner bit cuts a flat-bottom hole, but you can use any 1/2-in.-dia. bit.

Next, cut the 1/2-in. pine into strips for the drawer. The box shown has mitered joints, but you can assemble the drawer with butt joints if you prefer. (In that case, remember to adjust the dimensions.) Install the drawer bottom the same way you installed the box bottom, adjusting the size if you don't cut rabbets in the drawer sides. Glue the top in place and clamp it with C-clamps overnight. Finish with polyurethane or paint.

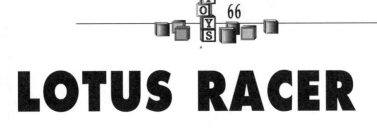
LOTUS RACER

Young racing fans will appreciate this toy race car modeled after a Ford Lotus. Metallic silver paint on the exhaust pipes, engine air scoop passages and wheel hubs makes the car look realistic.

"Drivers, start your engines," is a call that sparks excitement among racing fans of all ages. You can set a youngster's imagination in gear with this slick toy race car. It's loosely patterned after a Ford Lotus, and it's rugged enough to run many courses.

Because pine is easy to work, use it for all the parts except the dowel rods, which are birch. Poplar is another easy wood to shape, and it accepts paint well. If you plan to paint

LOTUS RACER

EACH SQ. = 1/2"

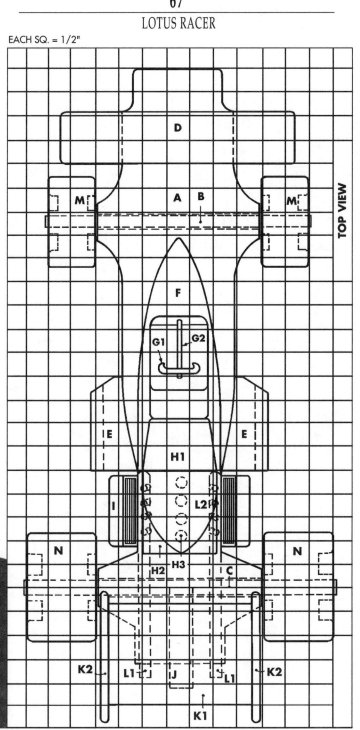

TOP VIEW

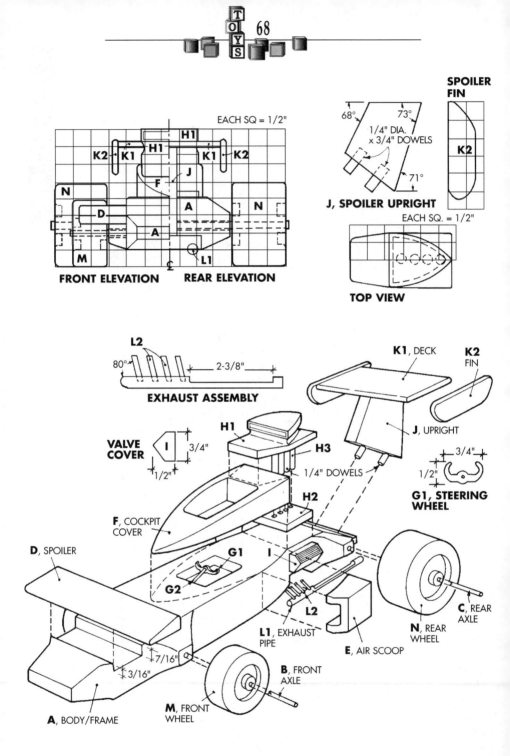

SPOILER FIN

EACH SQ = 1/2"

H1

K2 · K1 · H1 · K1 · K2

F J

N A N

D A

M A

L1

FRONT ELEVATION **REAR ELEVATION**

68° 73°
1/4" DIA. x 3/4" DOWELS
K2
71°

J, SPOILER UPRIGHT

EACH SQ. = 1/2"

TOP VIEW

L2
80° 2-3/8"

EXHAUST ASSEMBLY

VALVE COVER I 3/4" 1/2"

H1

H3

1/4" DOWELS

K1, DECK **K2** FIN

J, UPRIGHT

3/4"
1/2"

G1, STEERING WHEEL

H2

F, COCKPIT COVER

D, SPOILER

G1 I

G2

L2

L1, EXHAUST PIPE

C, REAR AXLE

N, REAR WHEEL

E, AIR SCOOP

7/16"
3/16"

B, FRONT AXLE

M, FRONT WHEEL

A, BODY/FRAME

LOTUS RACER

EACH SQ. = 1/2"

CUTTING LIST: LOTUS RACER
(all parts pine except dowels)

Key	No.	Part	Size
A	1	Body/frame	1-1/2 x 3-1/2 x 12-5/8"
B	1	Front axle	1/4" dia. x 5-5/8"
C	1	Rear axle	5/16" dia. x 6-5/8"
D	1	Front spoiler	7/16 x 1-1/8 x 5"
E	2	Air scoops	1 x 1-1/2 x 2"
F	1	Cockpit cover	1 x 1-3/4 x 5"
G1	1	Steering wheel	1/16 x 1/2 x 3/4"
G2	1	Steering shaft	1/16" dia. x 1-1/4"
H1	1	Engine air scoop	1 x 1-1/2 x 2-7/8"
H2	1	Scoop base	1/4 x 1-1/2 x 1-3/4"
H3	4	Scoop passages	1/4" dia. x 1"
I	2	Engine valve covers	1/2 x 3/4 x 1-1/2"
J	1	Rear upright spoiler	1/2 x 1-1/2 x 2-1/2"
K1	1	Rear spoiler deck	1/8 x 2-1/8 x 3"
K2	2	Rear spoiler fins	5/32 x 5/8 x 2-3/4"
L1	2	Exhaust pipes	5/16" dia. x 4-3/8"
L2	8	Connecting pipes	1/8" dia. x 7/8"
M	2	Front wheels	1 x 1-7/8" dia.
N	2	Rear wheels	1-1/2 x 2-5/16" dia.

Misc.: 1/4" dia. x 3/4" spoiler-body dowels (2); sandpaper; yellow glue; enamel paints.

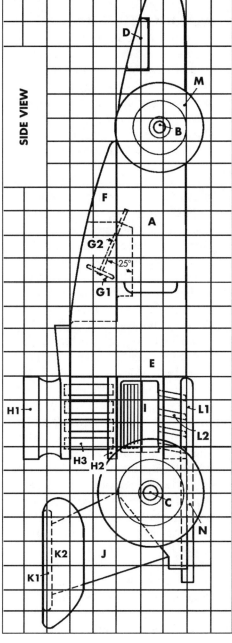

SIDE VIEW

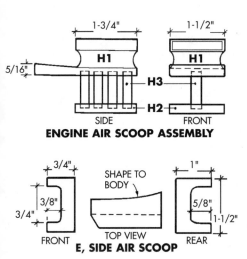

1-3/4"   1-1/2"

H1   H1

5/16"

H3
H2

SIDE   FRONT

ENGINE AIR SCOOP ASSEMBLY

3/4"   1"

SHAPE TO
BODY

3/8"   5/8"

3/4"   1-1/2"

FRONT   TOP VIEW   REAR

E, SIDE AIR SCOOP

the car with realistic multicolored markings, it's best to do so before assembling the parts.

MAKING THE BODY

To make the body **A**, use close-grained wood that's free from knots and other defects. Enlarge the patterns to make two templates: a top and side profile. Cut the body to size; then trace the patterns on the block. Cut the notch for the front spoiler with a band saw or circular saw with a fine-tooth blade. Turn the block over and cut the notch under the engine compartment.

Next, rout the cockpit cavity using a variable-speed rotary tool such as a Dremel Moto-Tool with a router attachment to smooth the bottom. Locate the axle hole centers on both sides of the body and draw a 3/4-in.-dia. circle (guidelines for tapering the axle housings) with a compass. Using a 1/4-in. brad-point drill bit, bore the front axle hole from both sides of the block for greater accuracy. Bore the rear axle hole the same way but with a 5/16-in. bit. Cut a 1/4-in. dowel **B** and a 5/16-in. dowel **C** for the axles slightly longer than is necessary.

Following the template lines, cut the side profile with a band saw. Tape the cutoffs back onto the block so you can follow the top pattern. Turn the block right-side up and cut along the template lines with the band saw. Now you're ready for hand trimming. Using a sharp knife, taper each axle housing to the 3/4-in. circle you previously marked around the axles. Sand smooth.

BODY PARTS

Cut the front spoiler **D** and trim it so that it fits in the notch but extends slightly above the top of the body. Glue the spoiler in place and sand it flush with the top.

Make the side air scoop blocks **E** and cut the U-shaped air passages with a band saw. Cut the angle on the leading edge of the scoop; then carefully cut it to fit the contour of the body. Glue one scoop to each side of the body and sand.

You'll need to make templates for the cockpit cover **F** with the cutout for the cockpit marked. The cutout in the cover is longer than the cutout in the body to create the driver's seat. Make the cutout in the cockpit cover with a scroll saw; then cut the sides and top to shape with a band saw. Sand the cover and fit it to the body, but don't glue it on yet.

Make the steering wheel **G1** from 1/16-in. stock and bore a 1/16-in.-dia. hole for the shaft **G2**. Glue the shaft in the wheel. Bore a 25-degree hole at the base of the cockpit and glue the steering assembly in place. Now you can glue the cockpit cover in place.

The engine air scoop assembly **H** comprises the scoop **H1**, scoop base **H2** and scoop passages **H3**, and it requires a bit more hand work than the other pieces. Cut the blocks for both the scoop and scoop base and make a top and side template out of paper. Trace the patterns onto the workpiece **H1**; then bore the 1/4-in.-dia. holes in both the scoop and the base for the scoop passages **H3**.

LOTUS RACER

Use a handsaw to remove most of the waste from around the arrowhead shape at the top; then use a band saw to shape the rest of the scoop. Refine the shape with a sharp knife and a round rasp. After sanding, glue the assembly together; then glue it to the body.

Cut the engine valve covers **I** and scribe the narrow grooves in the top with a carving tool, electric engraver or rotary tool. Sand the valve covers smooth; then glue them to the body.

Make the rear spoiler upright **J**, the spoiler deck **K1** and the spoiler fins **K2** with a band saw or jigsaw. Sand the parts smooth and drill two 1/4-in.-dia. holes in the bottom of the upright. Mark the corresponding holes in the body with dowel centers and drill the holes. First, glue dowels in the upright; then glue the upright to the body. Next, join the spoiler parts and glue the assembly to the upright. For added strength, drill small holes through the fins and the deck and insert toothpicks to act as dowel pegs.

The connecting pipes **L2** are set into the exhaust pipes **L1** at an 80-degree angle. Drill the corresponding holes in the body at a slight compound angle (about 5 degrees). Bore the holes freehand using a 1/8-in. brad-point drill bit mounted in a rotary tool. After making sure the dowels and the holes align, make the notch in the exhaust pipe dowels to conform to the body profile. You can carve, chisel or carefully cut the notch with a band saw.

WHEELS AND FINISHING

Cut the front wheels **M** from 1-in.-thick stock using a circle cutter or a hole saw. The drill bit in the center of the circle cutter makes a perfectly centered axle hole for a smooth-rolling wheel. Cut the recesses on the inside and outside of the wheels on a lathe. (Use a three-jaw chuck to mount the wheels on the lathe.)

Use the same method for making the rear wheels **N**. You may need to make cuts from both sides of the stock if the depth capacity of your circle cutter isn't adequate to cut through the stock at once.

Glue one wheel to each axle **A,B**; then slip each axle through the appropriate axle hole and position the second wheel without glue. Trim any excess dowel. Finally, glue the second wheel to each axle dowel.

The car shown in the photo was finished with clear satin finish to seal the wood and then coated with a flat white spray primer. After that, details were added with white, black, red and silver spray paints.

RIVERBOAT PUZZLE

his seven-piece steamboat puzzle is fun to put together, and kids will enjoy playing with the boat after they've assembled it.

To begin, enlarge the base half-pattern to full size and lay it out on 3/4-in. pine. Cut out the base and the decks and wheels using a band saw or sabre saw. (If you use a sabre saw, clamp a straightedge to guide the ripping operations.) Cut the curves freehand. To make the curves on the end of the decks identical, stack and clamp them so you can cut all three at once.

Next, make the cabin **H** from 1-1/2-in. stock (or glue together two 3/4-in. pieces). Cut a

6-in. length and make the curve cut on a band saw or clamp the piece to a table and cut it with a sabre saw. Then cut the cabin to length.

Stack decks **F** and **G** and drill the 3/4-in.-dia. holes for the smokestacks using a drill press or a hand drill with a drill guide. Use a backup board when drilling the holes to prevent splintering when the drill bit exits the work, and firmly clamp the workpieces. Next, drill two 1/4-in.-dia. holes for the cabin pins in the decks. Then drill two corresponding holes in the cabin. Enlarge the holes in the deck slightly by sanding with 100-grit sandpaper wrapped around dowels. This ensures that the parts will be easy to assemble even if the wood shrinks.

Sand all of the parts with fine-grit sandpaper and ease all sharp edges. Then fasten the lower decks **D,E** to deck **F** with glue and 1-in. brads. Now

Kids will have fun pretending to journey the great Mississippi River with this steamboat. When they tire of boating, they can separate the seven-piece puzzle and reassemble it.

RIVERBOAT PUZZLE

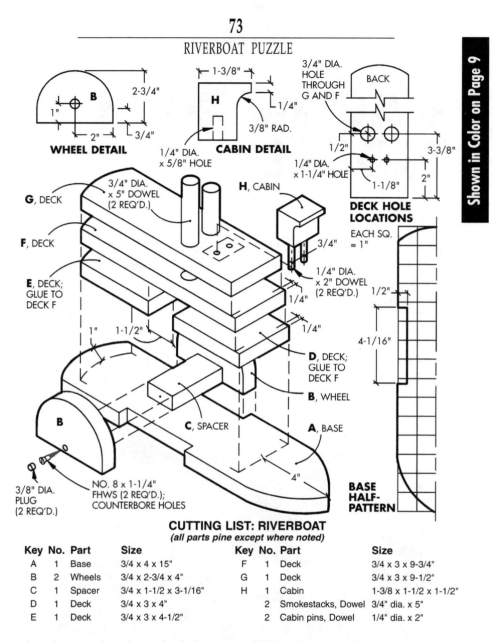

WHEEL DETAIL
2-3/4"
1"
2"
3/4"
B

1-3/8"
1/4"
CABIN DETAIL
3/8" RAD.
H
1/4" DIA. x 5/8" HOLE

3/4" DIA. HOLE THROUGH G AND F
BACK

1/2"
1/4" DIA. x 1-1/4" HOLE
1-1/8"
3-3/8"
2"
DECK HOLE LOCATIONS

EACH SQ. = 1"

G, DECK
3/4" DIA. x 5" DOWEL (2 REQ'D.)

H, CABIN

F, DECK

E, DECK; GLUE TO DECK F

1/4" DIA. x 2" DOWEL (2 REQ'D.)
1/2"
1/4"
1/4"
4-1/16"

1"
1-1/2"

D, DECK; GLUE TO DECK F

B, WHEEL

B

C, SPACER

A, BASE

4"

3/8" DIA. PLUG (2 REQ'D.)

NO. 8 x 1-1/4" FHWS (2 REQ'D.); COUNTERBORE HOLES

BASE HALF-PATTERN

CUTTING LIST: RIVERBOAT
(all parts pine except where noted)

Key	No.	Part	Size	Key	No.	Part	Size
A	1	Base	3/4 x 4 x 15"	F	1	Deck	3/4 x 3 x 9-3/4"
B	2	Wheels	3/4 x 2-3/4 x 4"	G	1	Deck	3/4 x 3 x 9-1/2"
C	1	Spacer	3/4 x 1-1/2 x 3-1/16"	H	1	Cabin	1-3/8 x 1-1/2 x 1-1/2"
D	1	Deck	3/4 x 3 x 4"		2	Smokestacks, Dowel	3/4" dia. x 5"
E	1	Deck	3/4 x 3 x 4-1/2"		2	Cabin pins, Dowel	1/4" dia. x 2"

glue the two dowels in the holes in the cabin.

Complete the paddle assembly by attaching the two wheels **B** to the spacer **C** with wood screws. Counterbore and plug the screw holes.

Sand the parts, easing the ends of all the dowels, and remove all glue squeeze-out. Check that all the parts fit together properly. Then separate the parts and apply several light coats of satin varnish, lightly sanding between coats.

WAGON WITH BLOCKS

ven novice woodworkers can build this toy wagon and set of blocks. Begin by cutting 1/2-in. pine into 2-in. strips for the sides **A**. Mark layout lines for the axle holders that protrude below the sides; then cut the sides with a coping saw, band saw or scroll saw. Bore 5/16-in.-dia. axle holes as shown on the Side Pattern.

Cut the short sides; then cut the bottom. Sand the parts smooth using 100- and then 150-grit sandpaper; then assemble the parts with glue and brads. Cut the wheels with a hole saw and sand them smooth. Cut the 1/4-in.-dia. dowel for the axles and put them in position; then glue the wheels to the axles.

Make the blocks from 5/4 pine (1-1/8 in. actual thickness). Cut two 2-in.-wide x 8-7/16-in.-long strips and one 2-7/16-in.-wide x 8-7/16-

Toddlers will have fun pulling around this pine wagon and playing with the blocks that fit inside.

WAGON WITH BLOCKS

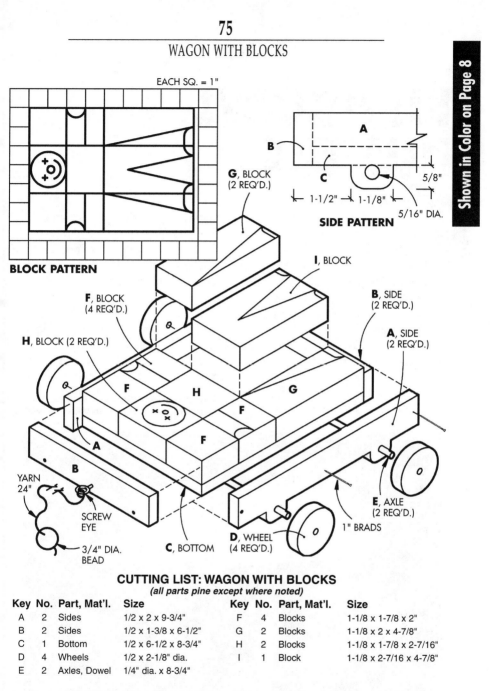

EACH SQ. = 1"

BLOCK PATTERN

G, BLOCK
(2 REQ'D.)

SIDE PATTERN

A

B

C

5/8"

1-1/2" — 1-1/8"

5/16" DIA.

Shown in Color on Page 8

I, BLOCK

F, BLOCK
(4 REQ'D.)

H, BLOCK (2 REQ'D.)

B, SIDE
(2 REQ'D.)

A, SIDE
(2 REQ'D.)

F

H

G

F

A

F

B

YARN
24"

SCREW
EYE

3/4" DIA.
BEAD

C, BOTTOM

D, WHEEL
(4 REQ'D.)

E, AXLE
(2 REQ'D.)

1" BRADS

CUTTING LIST: WAGON WITH BLOCKS
(all parts pine except where noted)

Key	No.	Part, Mat'l.	Size	Key	No.	Part, Mat'l.	Size
A	2	Sides	1/2 x 2 x 9-3/4"	F	4	Blocks	1-1/8 x 1-7/8 x 2"
B	2	Sides	1/2 x 1-3/8 x 6-1/2"	G	2	Blocks	1-1/8 x 2 x 4-7/8"
C	1	Bottom	1/2 x 6-1/2 x 8-3/4"	H	2	Blocks	1-1/8 x 1-7/8 x 2-7/16"
D	4	Wheels	1/2 x 2-1/8" dia.	I	1	Block	1-1/8 x 2-7/16 x 4-7/8"
E	2	Axles, Dowel	1/4" dia. x 8-3/4"				

in.-long strip. Next, cut each strip into three pieces according to the lengths shown in the cutting list. Sand and varnish the blocks and the wagon; then paint the design on the blocks.

Finally, install the screw eye in the center front of the wagon and attach the yarn and bead.

FISHBOWL PUZZLE

Children from about 18 months to 3 years old enjoy putting together simple puzzles like this one. All you need to make the puzzle is a 12-in. length of 1x10 pine (3/4 x 9-1/4 in. actual size) and a piece of 1/4- x 9- x 12-in. plywood. Equipped with a coping saw, handsaw, glue, paint and varnish, beginning woodworkers should be able to complete this project.

Begin by enlarging the pattern to full size; then trace it onto the plywood. If you are inexperienced at using a coping saw, practice on a scrap before you cut the actual puzzle. Keep the blade upright and do not force the cut. The blade should be well tensioned, not loose. Do not allow the workpiece to extend too far over the workbench. If the board vibrates excessively as you cut, the workpiece is extended too far.

Keep in mind that the kerf created by the saw blade allows enough clear-

Novice woodworkers can make this gift for novice puzzle solvers.

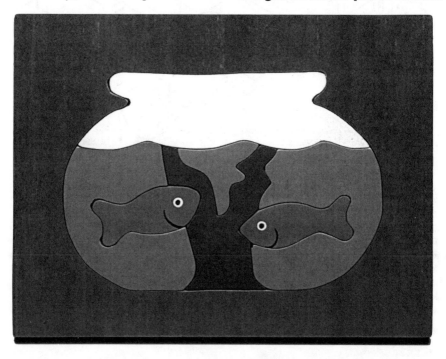

ance between parts. Drill a small starter hole at a suitable location (on any of the layout lines) on the puzzle pattern. Use a twist drill bit that will cut a hole just large enough for the saw blade to pass through. (To find the right size bit, drill test holes in a scrap before boring into the work.)

Clamp the plywood to the edge of a workbench and insert the coping saw blade. Then reattach the blade to the coping saw and cut out each piece of the puzzle.

Next, cut the 3/4-in.-pine base on a table saw or with a handsaw. Glue and clamp the puzzle perimeter to the pine base. After the glue has dried, sand the edges smooth. Then sand the individual puzzle pieces with 150-grit sandpaper. Make sure you sand the edges to eliminate all splinters and achieve a professional look. Wrap sandpaper around dowels or paint stirrers to sand irregular shapes. For a sculpted look, round over all of the visible edges.

Apply a satin polyurethane varnish to the base and paint the parts with latex enamel. Sand lightly; then apply a second coat of enamel.

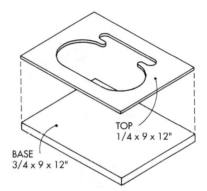

TOP
1/4 x 9 x 12"

BASE
3/4 x 9 x 12"

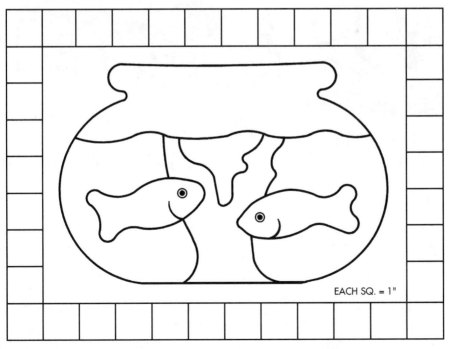

EACH SQ. = 1"

LITTLE HOUSE ON THE PRAIRIE

This freestanding puzzle makes a nice display in a child's room.

This freestanding six-piece puzzle is fun to put together, and when it's assembled, it can be used to decorate a shelf. Most of the pieces are cut from a 7- x 10-in. piece of 5/4 pine (1-1/8 in. actual thickness). The base is a 10-in. length of 3/4- x 3-1/2-in. pine.

Begin by enlarging the pattern and tracing it onto the stock. Using a scroll saw, cut the house, tree and lawn. Next, cut the house and the tree into two sections where indicated by the heavy lines in the drawing. Clamp the house, roof and base together and

LITTLE HOUSE ON THE PRAIRIE

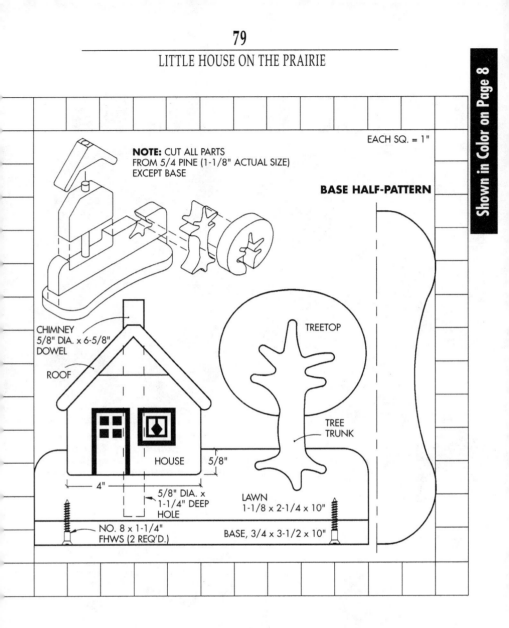

EACH SQ. = 1"

NOTE: CUT ALL PARTS FROM 5/4 PINE (1-1/8" ACTUAL SIZE) EXCEPT BASE

BASE HALF-PATTERN

CHIMNEY
5/8" DIA. x 6-5/8"
DOWEL

ROOF

TREETOP

TREE
TRUNK

HOUSE 5/8"

4"

5/8" DIA. x
1-1/4" DEEP
HOLE

LAWN
1-1/8 x 2-1/4 x 10"

NO. 8 x 1-1/4"
FHWS (2 REQ'D.)

BASE, 3/4 x 3-1/2 x 10"

drill the 5/8-in.-dia. hole for the chimney dowel into the base. Use a round file to enlarge the hole so that the chimney dowel fits easily.

Sand all the parts and paint them with acrylic. If you don't want the grain to show through, mix a bit of white with the colors. (This makes them more opaque.) When the paint is dry, attach the base to the lawn with glue and no. 8 x 1-1/4-in. flathead wood screws; then apply two or three light coats of spray polyurethane varnish to all of the parts.

LITTLE HAULERS

These tiny trucks are the perfect size for hauling Play-Doh cargo, and they're tough enough to withstand abusive young drivers.

▲ BOX-BED TRUCK

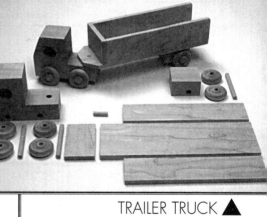

TRAILER TRUCK ▲

◄ FLATBED TRUCK

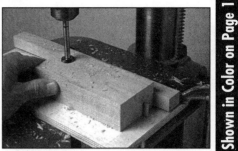

hese box-bed, flatbed and trailer trucks are easy to build. You can make one of each or mass-produce an entire fleet using the jigs on pp. 84-85.

1 *Start with the window hole. Put the dowel pin stop in the correct hole (see Drill Press Jig drawing, p. 84) for the cab stock you're boring. (The flatbed truck is shown.) Hold the stock firmly against the fence and the stop; then bore through.*

The trucks are made of 1/4- and 1-1/2-in.-thick maple, 1/4-in.-dia. dowels and 1-1/4-in.-dia. wheels (which you can buy from Woodworks, 4500 Anderson Blvd., Fort Worth, TX 76117; 800-722-0311). If you don't have a thickness planer to plane maple stock to 1/4 in., you can substitute 1/4-in. Baltic birch plywood or any other void-free plywood.

Although woods such as birch, poplar and pine are suitable for making the trucks, maple is the best choice because it is durable and it doesn't splinter easily.

2 *Repeat the procedures for the first step and bore the axle holes. Use two stop pins and slide the stock from one pin to the other to bore the axle holes.*

MAKING THE TRUCK BEDS

To start, cut all the 1/4-in.-thick truck bed parts from 1-1/2- and 2-1/2-in.-wide stock. First, rip long pieces to width; then cut them to length. (The front **B** is typical of all truck beds.) To speed crosscutting with a handsaw, cut one piece of each size to use as a template to mark the remaining pieces. If you use a table saw, clamp a small stop block to the saw fence on the infeed side of the blade as a guide. Adjust the fence so the distance between the stop block and the blade is the same as the length of the piece you're cutting. Use a miter gauge to push the stock through the blade.

3 *Cut the bed notch in the cab stock; then use the band saw jig to cut the windshield angle. The jig slides in the table's miter slot; hold the stock against the fence and the stop.*

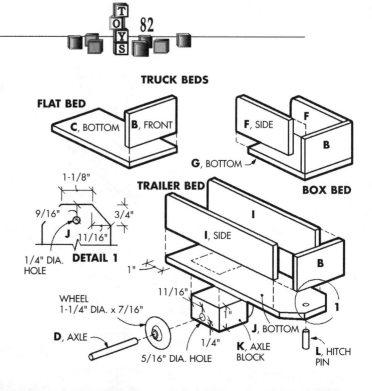

TRUCK BEDS

FLAT BED

C, BOTTOM B, FRONT F, SIDE F B G, BOTTOM

BOX BED

1-1/8"

9/16" 3/4" J 11/16"

1/4" DIA. **DETAIL 1** HOLE

TRAILER BED I I, SIDE B

1"

WHEEL 1-1/4" DIA. x 7/16"

11/16" 1" I

D, AXLE J, BOTTOM

1/4" K, AXLE BLOCK L, HITCH PIN

5/16" DIA. HOLE

4 Use the 45-degree angle block to cut the trailer bottom angles. (The blade guard has been raised for photo clarity.)

5 Bore the hitch-pin holes in the trailer bottom and the cab.

Before assembling the trailer parts, cut the angles on the front of the bottom **J** and bore the 1/4-in.-dia. hitch-pin hole.

Glue the truck beds or trailer together with white or yellow glue. Use masking tape or rubber bands to hold the parts together while the glue sets. After the glue has dried (about three hours), sand all the edges and corners smooth.

MAKING THE TRUCK CABS

Begin by cutting the truck cabs **A,E,H** to length. If you're using the

LITTLE HAULERS

TRUCK CABS

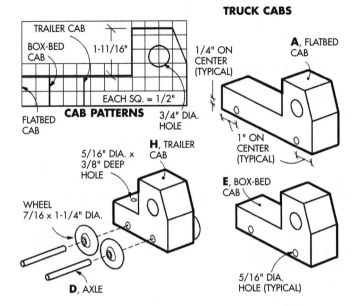

TRAILER CAB
BOX-BED CAB
1-11/16"
1/4" ON CENTER (TYPICAL)
A, FLATBED CAB
EACH SQ. = 1/2"
FLATBED CAB **CAB PATTERNS** 3/4" DIA. HOLE
H, TRAILER CAB
5/16" DIA. x 3/8" DEEP HOLE
1" ON CENTER (TYPICAL)
E, BOX-BED CAB
WHEEL 7/16 x 1-1/4" DIA.
D, AXLE
5/16" DIA. HOLE (TYPICAL)

CUTTING LIST: TOY TRUCKS
(all parts maple except where noted)

Key	No.	Part, Mat'l.	Size
Flatbed truck			
A	1	Cab	1-1/2 x 2-3/4 x 6"
B	1	Front	1/4 x 1-1/2 x 2-1/2"
C	1	Bottom	1/4 x 2-1/2 x 5"
D	2	Axles, Dowel	1/4" dia. x 2-3/8"
Box-bed truck			
E	1	Cab	1-1/2 x 2-3/4 x 5"
F	2	Sides	1/4 x 1-1/2 x 3-1/4"
G	1	Bottom	1/4 x 2-1/2 x 3-1/2"
B	1	Front	1/4 x 1-1/2 x 2-1/2"
D	2	Axles, Dowel	1/4" dia. x 2-3/8"

Key	No.	Part, Mat'l.	Size
Trailer truck			
H	1	Cab	1-1/2 x 2-3/4 x 3-3/4"
I	2	Sides	1/4 x 1-1/2 x 6-3/4"
J	1	Bottom	1/4 x 2-1/2 x 8"
K	1	Axle block	1 x 1-1/2 x 1-3/4"
L	1	Hitch pin, Dowel	1/4" dia. x 3/4"
B	1	Front	1/4 x 1-1/2 x 2-1/2"
D	3	Axles, Dowel	1/4" dia. x 2-7/16"

Misc.: 7/16 x 1-1/4" dia. wheels (see text for a mail-order source).

drill press jig, bore all the holes before cutting the notch that houses the cabs or trailer. Mark the window hole and axle hole locations. Bore the 3/4-in.-dia. window hole first. If you're using a hand drill, mark both sides of the cab and bore about halfway through the stock from one side; then complete the hole from the other side. Bore the 5/16-in.-dia. axle holes the same way.

Now you can lay out the notch; then cut it with a backsaw. Be sure to clamp the stock securely in a bench

vise. If you're cutting with a band saw, use a fence or clamp a straightedge to the saw table to guide the work.

Use the waste from the trailer cab notch to make the trailer axle block **K**; then bore the axle hole in it.

Next, mark the angle of the wind- shield on the front of the cab and carefully make a smooth cut. Now is a good time to bore the 5/16-in.-dia. hitch-pin hole in the trailer cab. Then sand the cab smooth, taking care to relieve all sharp edges and corners with sandpaper.

MAKING TRUCKS

The key to cranking out truck after truck is to use jigs — one for a drill press, the other for a band saw. A jig is simply an accessory that enables you to repeatedly perform the same function without having to measure and mark each workpiece. The jigs shown are custom designed for boring all the holes and making the angle cuts for this set of trucks. They are made of 1/2-in. plywood and hard wood scraps, but the type of wood isn't as important as how accurately you lay out the jig. Here are a few tips to help you make and use the jigs:

• Use the drill press jig shown below to bore all the axle holes and the window hole.

• For best results, use Forstner or brad-point bits for all drilling.

• The spacer beneath the fence on the drill press jig is cut narrow-

JIGS FOR BORING HOLES

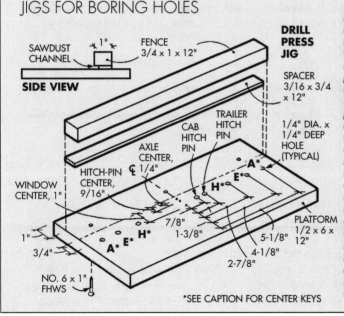

*SEE CAPTION FOR CENTER KEYS

LETTER KEYS: *The letters in the drawing at left coincide with the stop pin locations for the part being bored (see cutting list, p. 83). Use two stop pins to bore axle holes. After boring the holes in the cabs, cut the bed notches; then use the band saw jig to cut the windshield angle in the cabs and to make the angle cuts in the trailer bed. Measure from the band saw blade side of the jig to lay out the fences and the stop.*

ASSEMBLY AND OPTIONS

First, attach the axles and wheels to the cab and to the trailer axle block. The best way to do this is to dip one axle end into glue and put on a wheel. Then slide the axle through the axle hole and glue on the other wheel.

To complete the box-bed and flatbed trucks, glue the beds to the cabs. Finish the trailer by gluing on the axle block assembly and hitch pin.

You can paint the trucks with acrylic latex enamel or simply add details with a wood-burning pen.

PRODUCTION STYLE

er than the fence to create a saw-dust channel. This helps keep the corner between the fence and the platform clean.

• The first drill press operation is boring the window holes in each cab (photo 1, p. 81). Align the drill bit with the window hole in the jig; then clamp the jig to the drill press table. Realign the jig to bore the axle holes and the trailer hitch-pin holes.

• Note that there is no stop pin for boring the hole in the trailer axle block K. Butt the bottom of the block against the bed and bore 1 in. on center from the block's front edge.

• Use the band saw jig to cut the windshield angle on the cabs and the angles on the front end of the trailer bed bottom J.

• The band saw jig shown was designed for a 14-in. Delta model. The easy way to ensure accuracy with this jig is to first attach the guide (the bottom strip) to an oversize platform; then cut the platform edge with a band saw. Lay out and install the fences and stops after cutting the platform edge.

• Both jigs use dowel pins as stops. The band saw stops are glued in place; the drill press stops are movable.

JIGS FOR CUTTING ANGLES

BAND SAW JIG

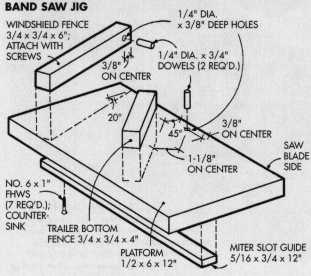

WINDSHIELD FENCE 3/4 x 3/4 x 6"; ATTACH WITH SCREWS

1/4" DIA. x 3/8" DEEP HOLES

3/8" ON CENTER

1/4" DIA. x 3/4" DOWELS (2 REQ'D.)

20°

45°

3/8" ON CENTER

1-1/8" ON CENTER

SAW BLADE SIDE

NO. 6 x 1" FHWS (7 REQ'D.); COUNTER-SINK

TRAILER BOTTOM FENCE 3/4 x 3/4 x 4"

PLATFORM 1/2 x 6 x 12"

MITER SLOT GUIDE 5/16 x 3/4 x 12"

STEAMROLLER

his big steamroller will pave imagi-
nary highways over carpets or sand-
boxes for years to come. It's beefy to
stand up to hard use, and it's easy to
make. The only tools you must have
to make this project are a table saw,
hand drill, sabre saw and coping saw.
Other tools that will help but that

aren't absolutely necessary are a
band saw or scroll saw, drill press,
router and disc sander. You could
turn the wheels, axles, smokestack,
barrels and headlights on a lathe, or
you can buy them from Cherry Tree
Toys Inc. (Box 369, Belmont, OH
43718; 800-848-4363).

*This heavy-duty
steamroller will hold up
to all the abuse a young road
worker dishes out. The simple
steering mechanism is easy for
little hands to operate. The roller
is made of six prefabricated
wheels glued together.*

STEAMROLLER

1 When cutting the pieces for the cab **A**, use a table saw with a sliding table to make accurate 90-degree cuts. A stop block ensures that all six pieces are exactly the same length.

START WITH THE BODY

Make all the pieces out of 3/4-in.-thick hard wood such as birch, maple or poplar. Begin by cutting to length six 5- x 9-in. pieces for the cab **A** (photo 1).

Next, cut a notch in the top front of each of the pieces for the hood to rest in (photo 2). Then bore holes through all of the cab pieces for two 1/4-in.-dia. dowels (photo 3). If you don't have a drill press or dowel jig that will locate holes on a wide face, clamp all the pieces together and bore through-holes with a drill (provided you have a long enough bit). Then glue and clamp the pieces together (photos 4,5, p. 90).

Now make the roller (photo 6). Orient the grain of all the wheels in the same direction or the layers will eventually delaminate.

MAKING FINGER JOINTS

The joints that make the yoke for the roller must be strong. You could simply butt the pieces together and drive two screws in each joint, but they will loosen with time. Finger joints are better and can be cut fairly easily on a table saw.

To make a finger joint jig, get two pieces of plywood or solid 3/4- x 4- x 15-in. stock. Screw one piece to your miter gauge at a 90-degree

2 To create the notch that the hood rests in, make a series of 1-1/4-in.-deep cuts very close to each other starting 4-1/2 in. from the end. Then knock out the waste with a mallet and clean up the notch with a sharp chisel.

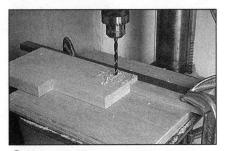

3 Use a drill press with a fence and stop block clamped to the table to accurately bore through-holes for dowels in each of the cab pieces. The dowels will hold the pieces in alignment when they're glued together.

HOOD ASSEMBLY

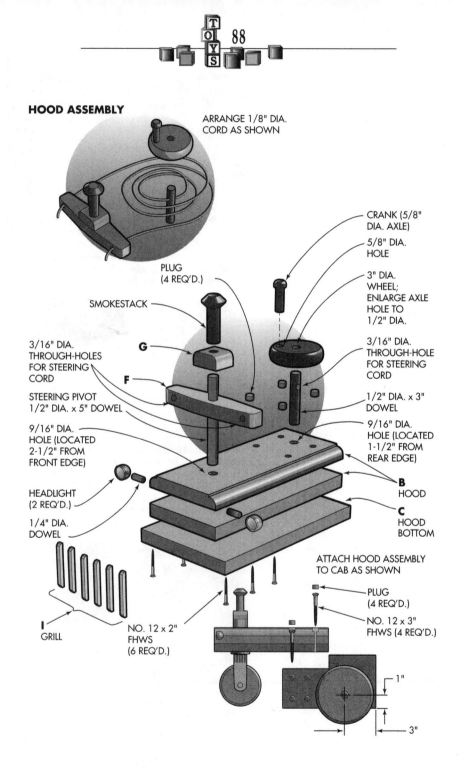

ARRANGE 1/8" DIA. CORD AS SHOWN

CRANK (5/8" DIA. AXLE)

5/8" DIA. HOLE

3" DIA. WHEEL; ENLARGE AXLE HOLE TO 1/2" DIA.

PLUG (4 REQ'D.)

SMOKESTACK

3/16" DIA. THROUGH-HOLES FOR STEERING CORD

G

F

3/16" DIA. THROUGH-HOLE FOR STEERING CORD

STEERING PIVOT 1/2" DIA. x 5" DOWEL

1/2" DIA. x 3" DOWEL

9/16" DIA. HOLE (LOCATED 2-1/2" FROM FRONT EDGE)

9/16" DIA. HOLE (LOCATED 1-1/2" FROM REAR EDGE)

B
HOOD

HEADLIGHT (2 REQ'D.)

C
HOOD BOTTOM

1/4" DIA. DOWEL

ATTACH HOOD ASSEMBLY TO CAB AS SHOWN

PLUG (4 REQ'D.)

NO. 12 x 3" FHWS (4 REQ'D.)

I
GRILL

NO. 12 x 2" FHWS (6 REQ'D.)

1"

3"

STEAMROLLER

CAB AND YOKE

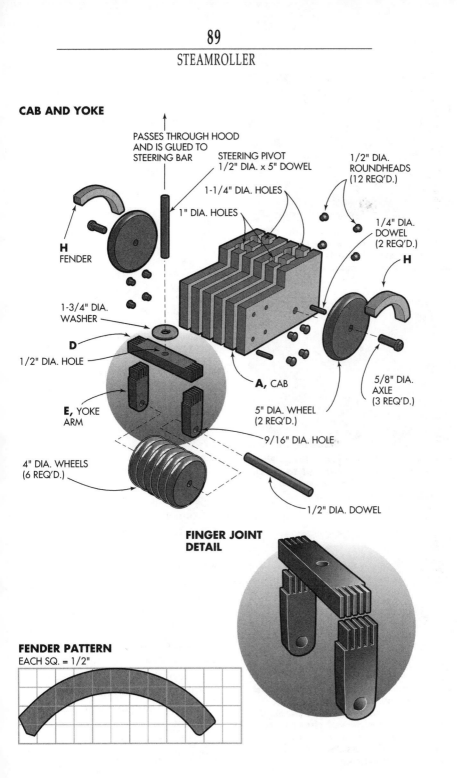

PASSES THROUGH HOOD AND IS GLUED TO STEERING BAR

STEERING PIVOT
1/2" DIA. x 5" DOWEL

1/2" DIA. ROUNDHEADS (12 REQ'D.)

1-1/4" DIA. HOLES

1" DIA. HOLES

1/4" DIA. DOWEL (2 REQ'D.)

H
FENDER

H

1-3/4" DIA. WASHER

1/2" DIA. HOLE

D

E, YOKE ARM

A, CAB

5" DIA. WHEEL (2 REQ'D.)

5/8" DIA. AXLE (3 REQ'D.)

9/16" DIA. HOLE

4" DIA. WHEELS (6 REQ'D.)

1/2" DIA. DOWEL

FINGER JOINT DETAIL

FENDER PATTERN
EACH SQ. = 1/2"

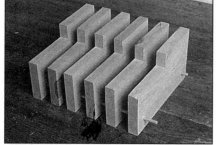

4 Wax the dowels and slide them through the holes in all six pieces. Leave enough space between the pieces to brush on glue.

5 After applying glue, clamp the parts together. Be careful to keep the parts parallel as they are pressed together or you could break a dowel.

6 Glue together six prefabricated 4-in.-dia. wheels to make the roller and insert a dowel through the center. The dowel should protrude about 3/4 in. on either side to function as the axle for the roller to turn on.

CUTTING LIST: STEAMROLLER
(all parts maple)

Key	No.	Part	Size
A	6	Cab	3/4 x 5 x 9"
B	2	Hood	3/4 x 5 x 11"
C	1	Hood bottom	3/4 x 6-1/2 x 11"
D	1	Yoke top	3/4 x 1-1/4 x 6-1/4"
E	2	Yoke arms	3/4 x 1-1/4 x 3-1/2"
F	1	Steering bar	3/4 x 1-1/4 x 6-1/4"
G	1	Steering bar	3/4 x 1-5/8 x 1-5/8"
H	2	Fenders	3/4 x 2 x 6"*
I	6	Grill	1/8 x 1/8 x 2-1/2"

*Use pattern in drawing to cut to shape.

Misc.: 5" dia. no. 313 wheels** (2); 5/8" dia. no. 301 axles** (3); 4" dia. no. 312 wheels** (6); 3" dia. no. 311 wheel** (1); no. 6 smokestack** (1); no. 54 headlights** (2); 1/2" dia. no. 103 roundheads** (12); no. 35 barrels** (2 — optional); no. 51 people*** (optional); 1/4" dia. dowel; 1/2" dia. dowel; no. 12 x 2" FHWS (4); no. 12 x 3" FHWS (4); glue; brads; latex paint; 1-3/4" dia. washer (1); 1/8" dia. cord (24" — cut to length).

**Can be purchased from Cherry Tree Toys (see text).

***Purchased from Cherry Tree Toys; trimmed to 2-1/4".

angle so that the cut will be about 6 in. from one end. Clamp the second piece to the first with two C-clamps. Raise the blade (a combination blade is fine) to 3/4 in. and cut a kerf in both pieces.

Remove the jig and put your rip fence on the saw. Rip a 12-in.-long piece of hard wood so that it is equal in thickness to the width of your saw kerf; then cut it to 2 in. long. Save the cutoff for later use.

Put the miter gauge and jig back on the saw. Remove the C-clamps and move the second jig piece to one side until the kerf in it is one kerf width away from the blade. Put

STEAMROLLER

the C-clamps back in place and insert the 2-in.-long piece in the kerf in the second jig piece.

Use the 2-in.-long reference piece to locate the cuts in the finger joint. One side of each joint begins with a finger, so the same side of the adjoining piece must begin with a kerf. To make this first cut, use the cutoff left over from making the 2-in. reference piece. Butt the cutoff up against the reference piece as in photo 7; then butt the work up against the thin piece.

7 *A homemade finger joint jig helps you make accurate cuts. To start the series of cuts with a slot rather than a finger, place a thin spacer between the short reference piece and the work.*

Before you cut your workpiece, practice on a scrap and adjust the distance between the reference piece and the blade so the fingers you cut fit snugly in the kerfs. Photo 8 shows the third cut being made in one end of a workpiece.

When you are able to produce a good joint that can be forced together with minimal pressure, cut finger joints in the yoke top **D** and arms **E**. Make both arms from one 3/4- x 1-1/4- x 7-in. piece — just cut the joints in both ends and then cut the piece in half. The kerfs that make the finger joints should be exactly 3/4 in. deep — the same as the thickness of the pieces.

8 *Here the second cut is placed over the short reference piece to locate the third cut.*

PUTTING IT ALL TOGETHER

Next, bore holes in the ends of the arms for the roller axle. Locate these holes so that there will be 1/8 in. clearance between the top of the roller and the yoke top. Slightly enlarge the holes in the arms so the axle turns freely by wrapping sandpaper around a dowel and rotating it in the hole.

9 *Glue the yoke pieces together with the roller in place. Use C-clamps to hold the fingers together to ensure a good glue bond.*

10 Use a router table with a 3/8-in. rounding over bit to shape the hood.

11 To fasten the cab and hood together, clamp them in a vise, drill counterbores and then drive four no. 12 x 3-in. flathead wood screws.

12 Cut out the fenders and then sand them smooth.

Round the ends of the yoke arms with a disc sander or cut them with a band saw, scroll saw or coping saw and sand them. Bore a 1/2-in.-dia. hole in the center of the yoke top for the pivot dowel. Glue and clamp the three yoke pieces together (photo 9).

Make the hood from three pieces **B,C**. Round over the side edges of the hood top using a router table (photo 10) or simply bevel the edges on a table saw. Clamp the three hood pieces in a vise and screw them together with four no. 12 x 2-in. flathead wood screws driven from the bottom and countersunk.

Remove the clamps from the cab and sand or plane the edges flush. Bore holes for the rear wheel axles and the ornamental round-heads, but wait to install them until after you've painted the body. If desired, bore 5/8-in.-deep x 1-1/4-in.-dia. holes for the barrels and 1/2-in.-deep x 1-in.-dia. holes for little wooden people to ride in. Bore 9/16-in.-dia. holes through the hood for the steering pivot and crank wheel dowels.

Next, screw the cab and hood together (photo 11). Fill the holes with wood plugs and when the glue is dry, sand them flush.

Using the pattern in the drawing, trace the fenders **H** onto 3/4-in. stock and cut them out with a sabre saw, coping saw, scroll saw or band saw (photo 12). Glue and clamp the fenders in place.

The crank wheel is made out of

a 3-in.-dia. wheel. Bore a hole for the crank, which is made from a 5/8-in.-dia. axle, and glue it in place. Enlarge the wheel's center axle hole to 1/2 in. and glue in a 3-in. length of 1/2-in.-dia. dowel. Bore a 3/16-in.-dia. hole through the dowel just below the wheel for the steering cord to pass through.

Next, cut the pieces for the steering bar F,G. Bore a 1/2-in.-dia. hole through the middle of part F for the steering pivot, and bore a 3/16-in.-dia. hole through the side of each end for the steering cord (see drawing). Bore a hole for the smokestack shank in part G; then glue part G to F and glue the smokestack in place.

The headlights are attached with pieces of 1/4-in.-dia. dowel. Bore a shallow 1/4-in.-dia. hole in one side of each headlight and glue in a short length of dowel. Bore corresponding holes in the hood, but don't glue the headlights in place until you've painted the body.

Cut the six grill pieces I and make a bevel in each end. Attach the grill to the hood with glue and brads.

FINISHING

Paint the body with two coats of latex paint. Sand lightly between coats. Glue the steering pivot in the hole in the yoke top and slip a 1-3/4-in.-dia. washer over the dowel. Pass the dowel through the hole in the hood and glue it in the hole in the steering bar. Then attach the wheels and glue on the headlights and roundheads.

Pass the steering cord through the hole in the crank wheel dowel and wrap each end of the cord around the dowel twice in opposite directions. Insert the steering wheel dowel in the hole in the body, but do not glue it in place or it won't turn. (The length of the dowel holds it in place.) Pass the cord through the holes in the steering bar and tie a knot in each end. Then order 10 yards or so of hot asphalt to be dumped in your front yard so your young contractor will have something to do with his new heavy machinery. Or just scuff up the carpet a bit and tell him it needs to be leveled out.

STEAM SHOVEL

Hard hats only! Here's a heavy-duty earth mover for sandbox contractors. For durability, it's made out of hard wood — maple, birch, poplar, oak, cherry and walnut are suitable. This project is a good way to use short scraps you've accumulated from other projects. You'll need a table saw, a hand drill, a coping saw, a plane and chisels. A drill press, planer, disc grinder and belt sander make the job easier, but you can build the project without them.

The wheels, axles, smokestacks and people are available from Cherry Tree Toys Inc. (Box 369, Belmont, OH 43718; 800-848-4363), or if you're looking for a challenge, you can turn them on a lathe. It's a good idea to buy or make these parts before you begin building the steam shovel to ensure the holes you bore for them will be the correct diameter.

MAKING THE BODY

Begin by ripping parts to width and then cutting them to length. Use a table saw with the miter gauge set up as shown in photo 1 for accurate cutoffs.

Bore the wheel axle holes in the two carriage sides **A** using a drill press (photo 2). You can also use a dowel jig to locate these holes, or simply align them by hand using a portable electric drill or a brace, but be careful to bore the holes perpendicular to the part face.

Use screws to assemble all the parts. To quick-

1 When cutting parts to length on the table saw, screw an auxiliary fence to the miter gauge to provide better support for the parts and to act as a base to clamp a stop block as shown. The stop block lets you cut duplicate lengths easily.

2 Bore the axle holes in the carriage sides on a drill press.

ly and easily drive screws, first bore holes and countersink them. Then drive the screws with a variable-speed drill/driver with a screwdriver tip. Be sure that the holes you bore are large enough so that the screws don't shear as you cinch them down. Use no. 8 x 1-1/4-in. screws throughout the project except for the base pivot screw.

Accurately locate parts as you screw them together by clamping them to each other (photo 3). A vise works for some joints; for others it's more convenient to use bar clamps. Screw together the carriage sides **A** and carriage front and back **B**; then screw this assembly onto the carriage top **C**.

3 Hold parts to be screwed together in a vise or with clamps so they stay aligned while you bore.

Use plugs to cover visible screws. You can make plugs at the drill press with a plug-cutting bit. Glue the plugs in the countersink holes above the screws. Wipe off excess glue with a wet rag. When the glue is dry, use a sharp chisel to

This rugged steam shovel picks up and dumps rocks, dirt and sand. The shovel scoops when the crank is turned; the lever releases the load.

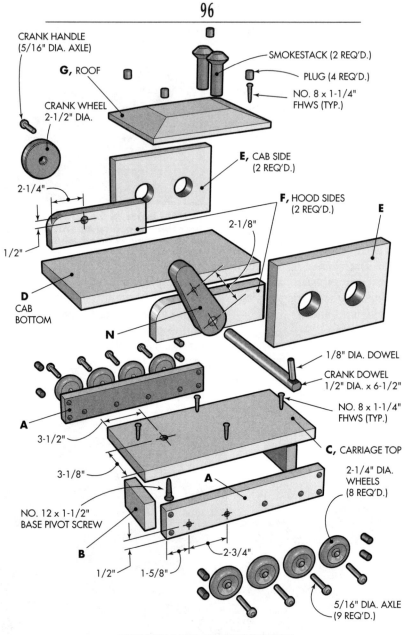

CRANK HANDLE
(5/16" DIA. AXLE)

G, ROOF

CRANK WHEEL
2-1/2" DIA.

SMOKESTACK (2 REQ'D.)

PLUG (4 REQ'D.)

NO. 8 x 1-1/4"
FHWS (TYP.)

E, CAB SIDE
(2 REQ'D.)

F, HOOD SIDES
(2 REQ'D.)

E

2-1/4"

2-1/8"

1/2"

D
CAB
BOTTOM

N

1/8" DIA. DOWEL

CRANK DOWEL
1/2" DIA. x 6-1/2"

NO. 8 x 1-1/4"
FHWS (TYP.)

A

3-1/2"

C, CARRIAGE TOP

2-1/4" DIA.
WHEELS
(8 REQ'D.)

3-1/8"

A

NO. 12 x 1-1/2"
BASE PIVOT SCREW

B

2-3/4"

1/2"

1-5/8"

5/16" DIA. AXLE
(9 REQ'D.)

CUTTING LIST: STEAM SHOVEL
(all parts hard wood)

Key	No.	Part, Mat'l.	Size	Key	No.	Part, Mat'l.	Size
A	2	Carriage sides	3/4 x 2 x 11-1/2"	F	2	Hood sides	3/4 x 2 x 6-1/2"
B	2	Carriage front/back	3/4 x 2 x 3"	G	1	Roof	3/4 x 6 x 8"
C	1	Carriage top	3/4 x 6 x 12-1/2"	H	2	Arm supports	3/4 x 2 x 11"
D	1	Cab bottom	3/4 x 6 x 12-1/2"	I	1	Arm	3/4 x 1-1/2 x 12"
E	2	Cab sides	3/4 x 4-1/2 x 7"	J	1	Shovel trap	1/2 x 3-1/2 x 4"

STEAM SHOVEL

SHOVEL ASSEMBLY

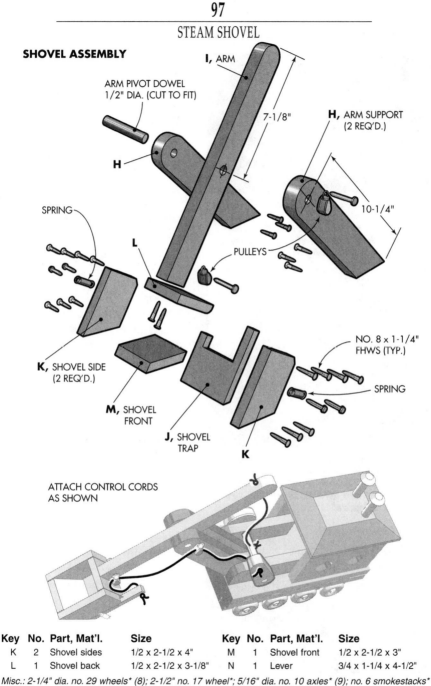

I, ARM

ARM PIVOT DOWEL
1/2" DIA. (CUT TO FIT)

7-1/8"

H, ARM SUPPORT
(2 REQ'D.)

H

SPRING

L

PULLEYS

10-1/4"

K, SHOVEL SIDE
(2 REQ'D.)

M, SHOVEL
FRONT

J, SHOVEL
TRAP

K

NO. 8 x 1-1/4"
FHWS (TYP.)

SPRING

ATTACH CONTROL CORDS
AS SHOWN

Key	No.	Part, Mat'l.	Size	Key	No.	Part, Mat'l.	Size
K	2	Shovel sides	1/2 x 2-1/2 x 4"	M	1	Shovel front	1/2 x 2-1/2 x 3"
L	1	Shovel back	1/2 x 2-1/2 x 3-1/8"	N	1	Lever	3/4 x 1-1/4 x 4-1/2"

Misc.: 2-1/4" dia. no. 29 wheels* (8); 2-1/2" no. 17 wheel*; 5/16" dia. no. 10 axles* (9); no. 6 smokestacks* (2); no. 22 people* (optional); no. 51 people** (optional); 1/2" dia. dowel; 1/8" dia. dowel; no. 8 x 1-1/4" FHWS; no. 12 x 1-1/2" FHWS (1); 1/8" dia. cord (40" — cut to length); 1/2" dia. pulleys (2); 5/16" dia. x 1-5/8" long springs (2); glue; latex paint.
*Can be purchased from Cherry Tree Toys (see text).
**Purchased from Cherry Tree Toys; trimmed to 2-1/4".

4 Cut 45-degree angles on the ends of the arm supports. Use an auxiliary fence for better support and a stop block as shown so that both pieces will be the same length.

5 When you clamp the arm assemblies to the base, insert the 1/2-in.-dia. arm pivot and crank dowels to ensure that the two assemblies are correctly aligned.

6 When cutting the beveled roof, attach a tall fence to your rip fence to support the part as the cut is made. Keep your fingers well above the blade throughout the cut.

level off the plugs.

Bore a hole in both the carriage top **C** and the cab bottom **D** for the main pivot screw that connects the two. Make the clearance hole in the cab bottom just larger than the screw shank so that the shank does not bind in it, and make the pilot hole in the carriage top smaller so that the threads grab tightly. Drive a no. 12 x 1-1/2-in. screw pointing upward through the bottom of the carriage top.

Bore 1/2-in.-deep x 1-in.-dia. holes in the cab bottom for the wood people to ride in using a Forstner bit or spade bit.

Next, use your miter gauge to cut 45-degree angles on the ends of the two arm supports **H** (photo 4). Bore 1/2-in.-dia. through-holes in the opposite ends of the pieces; then round off the ends with a disc sander or cut them off on a band saw, scroll saw or coping saw and sand them smooth.

Bore 1/2-in.-dia. through-holes in the hood sides **F** for the crank dowel. Round the front corner of the hood sides; then screw each of them to one of the arm supports. Clamp the two pieces together in a vise while you drive the screws. Use three screws in each joint.

Next, clamp the arm support and hood assemblies together on the cab bottom (photo 5). Locate the parts so that the arm supports are 13/16 in. apart.

Hold the cab bottom in a vise as you bore holes for screws through the bottom of the cab bottom into the hood sides. Use three screws in each piece.

Use a 1-1/4-in.-dia. spade bit to bore window holes in the cab sides. Butt the pieces up against a fence to ensure that the bit will not grab and spin the parts. You can also bore these holes with a hand drill. In this case, clamp the parts in a vise and place a back-up piece behind the hole to prevent tearout from the exiting bit.

Cut the bevels in the roof **G** on the table saw (photo 6). Screw the cab sides to the cab bottom (photo 7). Screw the roof to the sides in a similar manner, and use plugs to hide the holes in the roof. Use a drill with a spade bit to bore holes for the smokestacks in the roof.

MAKING THE SHOVEL

You'll need 1/2-in.-thick stock for the shovel. Plane stock to this thickness if you have a planer; otherwise resaw a 3/4- x 3-1/2- x 24-in. piece on a table saw (photo 8) or band saw. Use a hand plane or belt sander to smooth the rough face left by the saw blade. Cut to length one 4-in. piece for the shovel trap **J**; then rip the remaining stock to 2-1/2 in. wide for the shovel sides **K**, back **L** and front **M**, but don't cut it to length yet.

Cut out a 2-in.-deep U shape in the rear of the trap using a table saw with a sliding table

7 *Clamp the cab sides to the cab bottom and screw them in place.*

8 *To resaw stock on the table saw, locate the table saw fence 1/2 in. from the blade. Raise the blade 1 in. above the table and make a cut on each edge of the piece as shown. Next, raise the blade to 1-7/8 in. and make the two cuts again. Use a pushstick to complete the cut as the two parts are separated.*

9 *To safely make the cuts required on the end of the trap for the U shape, clamp the part to a fence like this one on a sliding table.*

10 *Angle the top and bottom edges of the shovel front M with a block plane or chisel.*

11 *Make relief cuts in the shovel sides so that the trap can open.*

12 *Remove the shovel front long enough to screw the shovel to the arm; then screw the front in place.*

(photo 9). You can also make this cut by attaching a tall auxiliary fence to your miter gauge. In either case, clamp the part to your fence because the part is too small to hold by hand safely. Move the piece incrementally to the side to clear out the middle of the U.

To make the two angled shovel sides **K**, cut 25-degree angles on the ends of the 2-1/2-in.-wide stock; then make cuts perpendicular to these ends. Cut out the shovel front **M** and back **L** and clamp the four pieces together. Note that the back protrudes below the angled sides to form the inner component of the trap hinge. Screw the pieces together, leaving the screws exposed for a rugged mechanical look.

Use a block plane or a sharp chisel to bevel the upper and lower edges of the shovel front (photo 10). Place the trap on the shovel and bore pivot holes through the fingers of the trap into the shovel back. Remove the trap and use a sharp chisel to cut clearances for the trap so that it can open (photo 11).

Cut the arm **I** to size, round one end and bore a 1/2-in.-dia. through-hole for the arm pivot dowel. Screw the shovel to the arm (photo 12). Cut one of the two trap fingers short and bore a 1/8-in.-dia. hole in the end of the other finger for the opening cord. Install springs on either

STEAM SHOVEL

side of the trap to hold it shut and pulleys to guide the cord to the release lever.

Make the crank from a 2-1/2-in.-dia. wheel. Bore a 1/2-in.-dia. hole in the middle and use a 5/16-in.-dia. axle for the crank handle. Glue the wheel to the crank dowel. Make the hole in the lever large enough so that it does not bind on the dowel. The dowel must not bind as it passes through the arm supports. Fasten the crank and lever assembly with the 1/8-in.-dia. locking dowel in the end of the crank dowel.

FINISHING

Before painting, remove the crank and shovel assemblies. Paint the body with two coats of latex paint, sanding lightly between coats. When the paint is dry, attach the smokestacks, wheels and crank and shovel assemblies. Finish the bare wood parts with a wipe-on oil finish; then attach the control cords as shown in the drawing. All that's left is to search your local toy stores for a little hard hat so your young contractor can break ground on that sandbox skyscraper right away.

Your Choice of

One of These 4 Popular Project Plans

Five Shop Jigs
WBH2095 $12.95

Red Wagon
WBH2052 $12.95

Five For the Birds
WBHBF5 $14.95

Freestanding Backyard Deck
WBH2070 $12.95

**MasterCard, VISA, Discover and American Express
Credit Card Orders Call Toll-Free 1-800-678-8025**

Use This Form to Order Your Free Project Plans and to Purchase Other WORKBENCH Plans or Books

Item #	Description	Qty.	Price
	(Your Choice)	1	FREE
	Total for Books and Products		
	Shipping and Handling		$3.00
	Missouri Residents Add 6% tax, Iowa Residents 5%		
	Total Enclosed		

Name

Address

City

State and Zip

Place order form in envelope and mail to:
**WORKBENCH Books and Products, Dept B95
P.O. Box 11230
Des Moines, IA 50340**